Blak to my Roots

WARNING: To peoples of Australian (Ab)Original and Torres Strait Island descent this book contains the names and images of deceased people.

By Steven Strong, Chris Thomson, Christine Walker, Meryl Mansfield, Unbulara, Darren McElroy, Nick Leidig, Peggy Rismiller, Mike McKelvey, Richard Bell, Dr Christine Gillies & Colin Watego

Published by Steven Strong, Chris Thomson, Christine Walker, Meryl Mansfield, Unbulara, Darren McElroy, Nick Leidig, Peggy Rismiller, Mike McKelvey, Richard Bell, Dr Christine Gillies & Colin Watego, 2024, Australia

Website: https://wirritjin-peggera-lin.au/home/

Email: ramindjeri@westnet.com.au

Phone: 0448 579 441

ISBN: 978-09945268-4-7

Copyright © Steven Strong, Chris Thomson, Christine Walker, Meryl Mansfield, Unbulara, Darren McElroy, Nick Leidig, Peggy Rismiller, Mike McKelvey, Richard Bell, Dr Christine Gillies & Colin Watego

First edition, 2024

All rights reserved. No part of this publication may be reproduced, stored in a retrieval system or transmitted in any form by any means, electronic, mechanical, by photocopy or otherwise, without the prior writer permission of the publisher and copyright holders.

Author: Steven Strong, Chris Thomson, Christine Walker, Meryl Mansfield, Unbulara, Darren McElroy, Nick Leidig, Peggy Rismiller, Mike McKelvey, Richard Bell, Dr Christine Gillies & Colin Watego

Title: Blak to the Roots

Subjects: history/ cultural studies/ archaeology/ anthropology/ spirituality/ indigenous studies/ Aboriginal Australia/ Aboriginal and Torres Strait Islander/ biography

Typesetting and design: Erica Schmerbeck

Technical Assistant: Evan Strong

Printed by: Ingram Spark

The Sign of Times

For I must thank my Ramindjeri Spirit
For my Mother the earth and I love her soul

My Father the wind was born free
Just like the air we still breathe

My sister the moon who can guide me through

And my Brother the sun who shines upon me

And my loved one the water
Who shall always be there
When needed the most

We live together as if we are one

You fellas out there
You still can learn
The secrets from the Old Ones

Karno Walker
The Warrior who walks between the two worlds

Contents

Introduction :
- Steven Strong 6

Chapter One:
As Close as we Could Get - Steven Strong 7

Chapter Two:
A Friend of Karno: Natural Historian and Conservationist
- Chris Thomson 24

Chapter Three:
Christine & Meryl - Christine Walker & Meryl Mansfield 27

Chapter Four:
A YOUNG MAN'S CAMP AT WULDE WAIIRRI - Nick Leidig . . . 35

Chapter Five:
Christine - Christine Walker 37

Chapter Six:
Unbulara - Unbulara 42

Chapter Seven:
Walking with Karno Walker - Darren McElroy 47

Chapter Eight:
Working With Karno - Nick Leidig 50

Chapter Nine:
SHARING CULTURE in the BUSH - Peggy Rismiller O.A.M. (Katerai:peri) &
Mike McKelvey O.A.M. (Nguridji) 54

Chapter Ten:
Spirit knows No Colour - Peggy Rismiller O.A.M.,
Mike McKelvey O.A.M. & Richard Bell 56

Chapter Eleven:

Planting Circles - Peggy Rismiller O.A.M. 58

Chapter Twelve:

In Memoria: The Teachings and Supervision Style of Karno Walker Who am I ? - Dr Christine Gillies 63

Chapter Thirteen:

In Conversation (Part 1) - Colin Watego & Steven Strong 75

Chapter Fourteen:

In Conversation (Part 2) - Colin Watego & Steven Strong 89

Chapter Fifteen:

Crossing the Divide - Steven Strong 98

Conclusion :

Steven Strong 102

Acknowledgements: 103

Introduction:

- Steven Strong

This book dedicated to Ramindjeri Elder, Law Man and Clever-fella Karno Walker, came about through a request agreed to by the Ramindjeri. It was Nick who first raised this idea, and his proposal was immediately accepted by many others. Because of the stature, standing and status of Karno, it was agreed by all this was a task beyond the capacity of any individual. In total there are eleven people who have contributed, for some a few pages were sufficient while others made a more substantial contribution. Regardless of volume, in the tradition of Wirritjin and Old Way Lore sensibilities, just as it was in the past when the results of a successful hunt were shared out evenly, all testimonies are of equal importance.

There is one inherent obstacle in this task we all had to negotiate. Karno is a Lawman, a Clever-fella, a magician par-excellence, an unmatched keeper of culture and is utterly unique by every standard. Putting such qualities and miraculous deeds into words is a brief none of us could satisfactorily grapple with. All we could cobble together is our best, but we do so with a caveat, Karno's Ramindjeri title means "lucky warrior: who walks between two worlds," and the only truth that comes out of this statement of fact and vocation is that none of the eleven have travelled as far down that mystical destination as Karno has.

So, limitations and restrictions aside, and in what only reflects the spirit and intentions of Wirritjin Karno spoke of constantly, there is an even spread of Original and non-Original witnesses who will offer their experiences and observations when in the presence of Karno. In closing our introduction, in the very simplest of terms we will, in one extended sentence, try and sum up what made Karno so important and so different from any other human we have met. He gave ceremonies to a variety of Heads of the Army, was introduced to the Governor Generals of South Australia and Australia, he was one the supervisors for the security in the Sydney 2000 Olympic Games, was called in to assist in the grading of black belts in various martial arts, a speaker of the First Language, a custodian of Sacred Original business, the companion of a pet dingo, he was the genuine Original version of Dr. Doolittle and a practitioner of Old Way magic

Chapter One:

As Close as we Could Get - Steven Strong

Over the last four decades I have met many Original Elders. For some the title is a self-proclaimed political statement that has little to do with cultural wisdom known and is more about a tally of grey hairs. For others, they are indeed worthy recipients of an acknowledgement of their knowledge of Original Lore. But beyond that there are three Elders where any such description falls well short of the mark.

The late Aunty Beve and Uncle Marbuck are Elders of the highest degree, their Original Lore pedigree is impeccable. But above and beyond their lofty station, stood Karno. From our perspective, which granted is subjective, we have never met anyone as immersed in Old Way sensibilities as Karno. From the first meeting, what stood out was that deep penetrating stare. It was something any on the receiving end fully agree that when he did focus on you there were no secrets, everything was exposed. So many others said exactly the same thing, they insisted that when he did really lock in on someone, their soul, and the deep inner secrets held within, were his for the taking.

Photo description: Karno on Kangaroo Island

Granted Karno has recently passed over, and while some critics may begrudgingly admit he was exceptionable in stepping beyond the realms of white-fella science, they would put this all down to being a relic of the past, an inconvenient historical possibility no longer relevant to the three dimensions of modern daily life.

Nine Inconvenient Truths

First up, it needs to be understood that what I witnessed while in the presence of Karno, all of it took place during this century, not hundreds of years ago, and most of what I will share occurred in the previous decade. And with two notable exceptions, every event was witnessed by not just me, but also by others who were no less astounded or bewildered.

It all started off somewhat innocuously, the first interaction I had with Karno was seemingly the least sensational, but ended up with a directive that certainly concluded with an excursion into celestial and mystical realms we knew so little of.

I was invited down to Ramindjeri country for a meeting, to discuss their claim that in very ancient times Original mariners circumnavigated to globe in a figure-eight formation, along with vague talk about some sort of ceremony. There was no mention of an agenda or return date, just come down and see what eventuates. Karno, and others, had read our first three academic books which were published by University Press of America and apparently that did meet with their approval, and that tick, along with Darren McElroy's recommendation, who was related and Ramindjeri himself, was sufficient to earn an invitation. But until I met them and won their trust, the details were still to be determined.

From my first meeting, nothing about this man was normal. We meet at a caravan park and at the time Karno oversaw an Original reburial that involved moving many Original skeletons from a site that was to become a bridge. Karno was the only person who knew the protocol and songs needed to move these bones to another appropriate location of his choosing. As impressive as this responsibility was, the dingo that sat with Karno never left my attention. I had never seen a domesticated dingo before, it was totally devoted to Karno. When Karno stood, so too did the dingo, and when he sat down the dingo was beside him.

On one occasion when we were sitting together, with the dingo next to his feet, three dogs wandered over at different times, and in each instance, it was clear they wanted the dingo to engage in play or some sort of doggy-activity. Twice the dingo never moved but did give the approaching canine a deep penetrating stare (something Karno was renowned for) and on both occasions the dogs backtracked with their tail curled between their legs. On the third visit the dingo did begin to stand, and I suspect the tacit invitation was accepted, but then Karno also rose, and the dingo followed him, and the other dog immediately backed off. It was so clear, the other dogs looked upon the dingo as if it was royalty, whose only loyalty and allegiance was to Karno.

Seven days had passed before Karno came up to me and grabbed the black folder I kept my notes in, and literally threw it away stating that, "You won't need this." He handed to me an incredibly decorated sacred stick and told me to hold it. He told me the stick would decide if I was deserving of ceremony, then left me to my own devices. I held that stick for over an hour before Karno returned; he took the stick off me then declared that I had met with its approval. Karno, along with Peter Mansfield-Cameron, Bluey and other Elders whose names I have forgotten, sat in a circle and sung in language with Karno singing and at times whispering instructions into my ear.

After the ceremony Peter sat beside me and told me that soon I would go out into country to examine a series of astronomical sites. I told him I knew nothing about astronomy, I could not even identify where the Southern Cross or any well-known constellations were. My self-confessed celestial ignorance did not deter, as he insisted it made no difference. About three weeks later he rang me and told me it was time to investigate, but I made the point I knew nothing about the stars and nor did we have any such sites to investigate. He laughed insisting that "you will, soon enough." Two days later the Senior Park Ranger for both the Snowy Mountains and Brisbane Waters rang offering to take me to both locations to examine a variety of archaeological sites, beginning with two massive astronomical constructions found in the Snowy Mountains.

Eight Hawks, a Figure Eight and new Horizons

It took close to six private meetings with the farmer who owned the Standing Stones site, before he agreed to allow a team under my supervision two days on site investigating and recording the rocks, mounds and sundry artefacts. We met below the farmhouse, there was a big mob of close to forty people in the group and there was an even mix of Original and non-Original people. There were ten Original Elders, and after some rather animated meetings beforehand it was agreed that Karno would have the final word on all matters pertaining to culture and spiritual pursuits. We left the rest behind as first up we had to get the Guardian Spirits to agree to our presence on such a sacred site, and until that happened, or didn't, there was no way any archaeology would take place. Such important business must observe Old Way protocol.

Photo description: Screenshot taken from a documentary about "Australia's Stonehenge" where Karno was performing ceremony near this "Standing Stones" site.

It was about one-and-half kilometres to the site, and as we got closer Karno and others called out to the "Old Ones" explaining why we were coming. Once arriving at the two mounds we split up, and a smaller group went over to the smaller mound (seventy metres long x ten metres wide x three metres high), while most followed Karno who took them up to the much larger mound upon which the 184 Standing Stones were originally positioned. At a site where the southern circle of stones once stood, Karno took up the same position then broke into song. No-one recognised it, but with benefit of hindsight and knowledge of the contents of an unexpected letter in the post that turned up a few years later, we strongly suspect he was singing in the First (Soul) Language.

That may well explain why so many hawks replied to Karno's invitation to attend and circle. It began with two hawks appearing in synchronicity from two different locations yet forming up a joint circle directly above Karno as he kept singing. It was not even close to a minute past their arrival before three more hawks had answered his call and joined into a much larger circular formation above. No-one spoke or to be honest was capable of doing so, there were no words that came close, but three more hawks did get much closer to the source. In fact, whether the number of birds was too great in navigating a single circle or that geometry was insufficient for this ceremony can never be known. But the eight hawks were now gliding in a figure eight formation and that required crossing intersecting paths through cooperative thinking or direction. Either way the hawks remained in that flight path for at least another minute. The time between when Karno finished singing to when the formation scattered was just one second if that. There is absolutely no doubt that these wild birds came from all over for no other reason than it was the song Karno sung, of which the lyrics are Soul Language, and that response of the hawks of such numbers and synchronicity gives us a clue as to how powerful the words of this language could be.

It is not a natural event for wild hawks residing in wetlands and rainforest, who are solitary hunters, to flock together then circle around an area lacking in any food source, that has never been recorded or seen anywhere. What I do know as a truth is that if that same event happened in ancient times and was recorded in the Bible, it would be referred to as a miracle, an action that is beyond the understanding of human science but is still real, because it happened in front of five witnesses.

That Night Around the Open Fire

That night as we sat around the fire-pit, more than once I was asked to question Karno as to how he got all these birds to not only come but fly in the sacred formation that represented "infinity." My negative response was consistent and based on a track record of never getting the answer I expected whenever I asked or was asked a question by Karno. Anyway, Karno had another agenda that night, he wanted to inquire, not reply, and I was his prime target.

Throughout the night he peppered me with a series of questions I had no idea how to answer. The laughter delivered with that customary mischievous grin he was known for was constant, he had no time for what happened hours before. I do remember one of our friends, Paul, came up to me looking a touch distressed as he offered his condolences and wondered why Karno was attacking me with such relish.

No, no, no it was an honour. His assumption that these were critiques was way off the mark. That he spent so much time trying to share knowledge with me is an honour gratefully accepted. I asked him how many times Karno asked him a question, to which he correctly replied, "none." What he did not know was that whenever Karno wished to speak to me, another would ring me informing me that I had to ring him. With one exception I really did not fully comprehend what he was sharing with me, and on that one occasion I proudly responded in the positive, all he could offer in response was "well it is about time."

As to how he actually called the hawks, no-one asked and no-one has any idea beyond that he definitely was solely responsible, and that is the way it should be.

The Final Step

If it was just the hawks, all of this performance could just be an incredibly rare display of group aerobatics, but there is more, much more, and of the four mystical events Karno created that we have chosen, what he did in front of nine people was certainly the most dramatic and theatrical.

When Graham Hancock came to Australia for a series of presentations, he contacted us asking us as to whether we would take him on country to see some of the sites and archaeology we have investigated. We agreed to do so under one condition, in that after the six days looking at sites along the east coast of Australia, he would do ceremony with Karno on Karta (Kangaroo Island).

Photo Description: (for above and 2 photos below): journalist, researcher and author Graham Hancock trading knowledge.

Photo description: *Karno and Graham observing Graham's wife Santha taking a photo of cultural artefacts.*

I had no idea what Karno had planned for Graham and his wife Santha, and when he first appeared done up Old Way with white ochre body markings, a lap-lap and his red bandana wrapped around his forehead, I knew that whatever he was going to do, it had begun. He stepped down into the firepit and started talking and singing, primarily in Original language, as to whether it was Ramindjeri or Soul Language was unknown. It wasn't so much what he said, which was undeniably important, but what he did upon exiting. The first step out was clear and precise, but the second step backwards breached the divide-he disappeared! He was totally gone, I glanced across to Graham and his mouth was open, but nothing was coming out, he like all of us, was speechless.

For no less than a minute no-one spoke and no matter which way we looked, he was still missing. Then out of nowhere, he stood behind his wife Christine and had that huge grin plastered across his face, as he surveyed the stunned looks. I do remember that a few of the party pleaded with me to ask him what he did and how. As before I refused, knowing that whatever the answer was it would be cryptic and totally obscure. However, someone did ask the day after, and the answer was surprisingly unambiguous. What he said was that there was a curtain he stood behind for a while then came back. It was no big deal as that curtain/portal was always there for anybody to use, all they had to do was learn how to look properly.

I remember sometime after asking another Ramindjeri Elder, Wirritjin, about this apparently miraculous event, and was slightly taken aback by his description of this as a "party trick." It is not that he was dismissing and casting doubt on what Karno did, but just giving it the proper perspective. What Karno did catch our attention for sure, but disappearing does not provide extra food on the table, create shelter or make something. It is purely entertainment with the potential to expand horizons and give us something to remember and talk about. The reality is that there were nine people who saw this and all neither question nor contend that it was real in every sense, and that what happened was clearly positioned outside the laws of white-fella science.

The Removalist

Not long after Graham's visit/ceremony Christine rang me passing on Karno's need for me to ring him. Normally she gives no clue as to what he wanted to talk about, but this time around was different as she did mention that he was concerned about Ros' Rock 1.

When I rang, he began by asking whether Ros' Rock 1 was in the house. It was a question that seemed a touch odd as I had kept him fully up to date with every rock either bought or found by others, and all archaeology conducted, and until now he had never asked for more details or placed any restrictions on what we did. I answered in the affirmative as that rock and some others were indeed safely secured in the house.

He made it clear that the rock was now more active, and it was dangerous for humans to be in close contact, and it had to moved outside. In adding to this request to reposition, he shared with me the Dreaming story associated with this rock which I think was given to help emphasise the importance and power of this rock. Karno was adamant that the engraved narrative on this rock was all about Aliens in the form of the goanna totem who wanted to meet and greet the Original people but were thwarted by the human crow and eagle totems. And that impasse continued until the crow switched sides once realising that it would benefit both groups if they ceased hostilities and joined together.

Eagles Watch

It was around three months after Karno suggested that the rock vacate our premises when I came down to Karta for reasons I can no longer recall. Equally, as to why I was driving a small bus around the island is no clearer, but past these unknowns what happened once we were all seated inside the bus will never be forgotten.

Karno was sitting beside me as he knew where he was taking us and I didn't, but right now his focus was not down on the ground but way up in the sky. As was mine, because directly beside me, at eye level was a wedge-tailed eagle flying at the same speed as the bus.

It was no more than two metres from where I sat and maintained that positioning for over a minute. As did the eagle next to Karno, same height and speed as its compatriot, and all the time this happened Karno never stopped softly singing. Everyone in the bus was totally absorbed by the sudden appearance of the two eagles and equally, were fully aware of who sung them up. As it was at the Standing Stones site, the second that Karno stopped singing so too did both eagles fly away.

For maybe a few seconds I did entertain the thought of asking for an explanation but after Karno ceased singing that customary mischievous grin was plastered across his face, and I knew if I asked the reply would be something entirely enigmatic. Moreover, this was merely an entrée because we had now arrived at the first site Karno had chosen, and there standing on the beach waiting for Karno was a wedge-tailed eagle. Whether it was one of two that escorted us to this site, or a new entrant was unknown, but once we stopped Karno went over to the massive bird and sat beside it as we waited some distance away. They spent no less than three minutes in silent congress, and once Karno stood the bird departed.

      Not a word was said by us, as Karno said nothing about their meeting and was more concerned about taking us to a site further along the beach. Not long after we were at the location Karno chose, and for reasons unknown yet again, it was just me and Karno together and the rest of the group were a couple of hundred metres away.

      Karno asked me what the arrangement of rocks about thirty metres from the shoreline was, and my response was both immediate and this was the second time I actually knew I was correct. "A rock fish trap."

      Finally, I got something right, but I never expected Karno's response.
      "You better go and check it out."

      "What? Walk out there? I'll have to take off my shoes and jeans first."

      "No need, just walk out there and make sure that it is a fish-trap."

I was about to explain why I needed to remove my shoes and jeans, but one look into his eyes and the broad grin that accompanied, and I knew what had to be done. The beach faced south which meant the currents came from Antarctica, and even though I had the added protection of denim jeans and canvas sandshoes, it helped little, it was so cold. As I went further into the water the rest of the group had returned and taken up spectator positions and clearly found my journey into the deep amusing.

With a towel on the seat and saturated jeans and shoes driving the bus became somewhat moist, but within two minutes after departing the beach two more eagles were first spotted by Karno. He told me to stop the bus, so as to not disturb or distract them. After all, how many times have I seen two wedgetails mating? They were on a fence post close to the road, and for the next two minutes we waited until they finished and flew away.

We then made our way up a hill and upon reaching the crest we saw three men staggering out of an upturned badly damaged four-wheel-drive. The car was a mess and that all three were relatively unharmed was hard to fathom, but when talking to them there was something even more amazing and personal to absorb. From what they said, if we had not been stopped by the eagles, we may well have been rounding that same corner from the opposite direction, at the same time the driver lost control. When factoring in three eagle appearances leading up to the crash, it seems extremely likely none of this was coincidental but was providential, especially since Karno's totem is the wedge-tailed eagle.

The First Rock Ceremony at Karta

Maintaining the same chronological order in our selection of Karno's science and magic, the next event was close to a year after the eagle's multiple performances and took place at the Culture Centre at Karta (Kangaroo Island). There was a three-day fire ceremony, and I was asked to bring as many of the sacred rocks I could to be part of the ceremony.

Photo description: Steven Strong discussing the importance of the Sacred Rocks he brought to Kangaroo Island (photo is screenshot taken from Louise Clarke's YouTube Channel)

All up two suitcases carrying 25 kilograms each was as much as I could bring. The rocks were placed to the side of the fire pit and stayed there for the three days, and unbeknownst to me at the time, this all had immediate consequences.

What was also being addressed with these rocks was strict adherence to Original protocol and sacred business. It was Karno who first suggested this and was very keen to see it come to pass. He wanted all the rocks secure and open to public access in Ramindjeri tribal land with the Karta (Kangaroo Island) Culture Centre, which he managed, being the proposed Keeping Place. As Evan, Ros Mulder and I agreed to Karno's request, it was decided that around fifteen rocks would stay with Karno, and once arrangements had been made to safely store and display all the rocks, the rest would join them. While the humans may have reached a consensus, not so the rocks. Karno accepted the fifteen rocks, knowing more were to come later, but I was never sure that the rocks were agreeable to a multi-staged agenda.

Karno is totally Old Way, from that perspective I am so far from where he is. He knows the songs, the Soul Language from which all other languages evolved, and he reeks of protocol, it drips out of every pour of his skin. He along with so many other Elders have assured me that I will be able to unlock the secrets and latent energy within these rocks, but the truth was at that stage my progress was minimal as the rocks were still sussing me out. To begin I didn't know their protocol, whereas Karno surely did, but the point was I knew they would respond favourably to him immediately. It was like going home for them, while with me the jury was still out. For the rocks protocol is everything, and I just knew that so many rocks which were returning with me were not happy because Karno is completely and utterly Old Way and I'm merely a student at best. They knew their time on Ramindjeri land would come, but right now that didn't count for much because the rocks given to Karno would be hidden and will remain so until the buildings and display of rocks in formation will be safe and protected. Irrespective of which rocks stayed or returned, just under two hundred were carefully wrapped and packed into the two suitcases.

I just managed to get a seat on the last plane out of Adelaide which got to Sydney very late, way too late to get a flight to Byron Bay. So, I booked a room in a cheap hotel/motel simply because it was so close to the Domestic Airport, and since I had two suitcases with forty odd kilograms of rocks inside to drag along, a distance of 800 metres made a booking there obligatory.

I had a poor night's sleep with the rocks in the unit, they and I just could not settle down. The only benefit was that I was up early for the flight, but crossing the only main road between the motel and airport was a daunting task. The flow of traffic just never seemed to stop and with no pedestrian crossing nearby, I figured eventually there would be break in the traffic caused by stop lights somewhere close by. After over five minutes waiting, I did see up ahead what seemed to be a gap. Fortunately, the driver of a semi-trailer could see me and seemed to be waving his hand across which I took as an invitation to quickly proceed.

With both wheeled suitcases at my side, I felt the gap was sufficient, but after taking two steps onto the road as my left foot was preparing to continue forward, it felt like I was 'ankle tapped.' When playing football and running past a defender and seemingly out of reach, the person passed sometimes dives to ground and reaches out with the closest hand in an attempt to flick the ankle so that the player carrying the ball stumbles and then falls. Well, I wasn't playing football as such but something with considerable force pulled my ankle, and I fell face first onto the bitumen. I let go off the bags and extended my hands in attempt to cushion the impact of the fall, but first up my main concern and focus was the truck that had its brakes applied and was swerving as it got closer. I could see both the smoke and expression on the driver's face, strangely enough everything seemed to slow down, and as the wheels got much closer the main issue was whether it could stop in time, because I was now laying in a position where the truck was heading towards.

It did stop, no more than two metres from where I was still lying. Both hands were bleeding and my left-hand had a large chunk of flesh missing, which has since grown back but is decidedly lighter in flesh colour to this day. My cheek and forehead had hit the road and was also bleeding, but when it came to more serious damage I was in reasonable shape. I picked up both bags and got off the road which saw the traffic pick up speed. The two hankies I found did a reasonable job of stopping the flow of blood. Turning up two minutes later with a torn bloodied shirt, plus hankies wrapped around both hands at the counter to get my baggage checked, certainly got quite a few second glances.

The rocks tripped me, of that there is no question. This was their way of voicing their displeasure and reminding me that they have the final say. My suspicion was they knew I would survive, and this was their way of letting me know who pulls and trips the strings. The only definite that can be taken out of their protest was that if they had not met Karno, my hands, cheek and forehead would not be shredded and bleeding. However, they also knew the Culture Centre needed funding and extensions, and further on very soon after Karno passed over the entire complex was White fella legally stolen from the Ramindjeri and they were literally evicted from the island. So, putting all the rocks on the island then would have been a disaster, and those that were left behind have been hidden ever since.

From my first meeting with Karno and Christine until some rocks were left behind at Karta spanned a nearly a decade, and when I wasn't visiting in South Australia, I stayed in contact with Karno via the phone. Normally it was Christine that would ring alerting me to the need to ring Karno as he had something to share, and these phone calls were never more than three weeks apart. So even though much of our contact was not face-to-face, it was the next best alternative, and it meant all our archaeology in the field was always discussed and analysed by Karno. If an error in protocol or procedures did occur, which was not often, Karno would always point out my mistake and the measures that needed to be taken to remediate.

Then everything changed when he passed over.

The Rock Workshop in Adelaide

This was first time I had come back to Adelaide since Karno had died, and from my stance I had no good news to share. Despite all the assurances over how I will lock into the rock's inner secrets, my mystical cupboard was bare and as for changing this non-state of affairs, I had nothing beyond a request I did expect to be denied.

Photo Description: Steven Strong (standing) discussing the sacred rocks while at his Adelaide Workshop

From the time Karno first knew of the increasing ensemble of sacred rocks, he was absolute in his directive that no-one but me could ever touch rocks like these. To do so, from his perspective, was a 100% guarantee of grief or much worse. The reason why Evan and I came this time was to put on a rock workshop at the Irish Club in Adelaide. The recurring issue was that at a superficial level I had plenty to say in regard to the evidence apparent on the surface of these rocks which could never come about through any application of stick, stone and bone technology. That was easy, but when it came to the inner secrets, the power and magic residing within, I had nothing bar the clues Karno gave me in relation to Ros' Rock 1.

The only solution I could offer to this impasse was to allow the Original Elders who had come to the workshop to hold the rocks and see what eventuated. There were about 60 people in attendance and quite a few were Original, which was an encouraging first step, but as to whether any could actually touch the rocks, well that was a moot point and one I raised with the Ramindjeri Elders. I spoke to a group of five Elders explaining my predicament which in practical terms meant I had half the content needed to make this the daylong event it was advertised to be.

After explaining why I wanted to contravene Karno's edict the Elders said they would discuss the matter privately and let me know what their decision was. As I began the presentation, I explained why I asked for an exemption, and at that stage Unbulara rose and announced that after careful consideration they had decided Karno's ban on anyone but me touching these rocks still stood and under no conditions would that be annulled. My immediate reaction was simply that I just did not have the content to last a full day and I was pondering over announcing a partial refund as the presentation began. Just as I was going to interrupt my opening explanation as to the abridged timetable, Unbulara stood and asked for permission to speak on Karno's behalf. She said that Karno just made contact with her and told her that until midday anyone, irrespective of colour, can hold the rocks.

Three people immediately volunteered, and in what was a reflection of Wirritjin, all three were non-Original. But there was much more to this day, the rocks were literally charged up and turned on and no-one doubts for a millisecond that this was also at Karno's initiative. Three different people brought measuring devices called tri-field meters and the needles on all three were reaching the maximum level as they were held over individual rocks. Many of the rocks that reacted were somewhat plainer and less dramatic in presentation, it really was a totally unexpected and welcome change in circumstances.

One particular reaction shocked all of us, and in particular Chris Blackmore who held his hand above the speckled white grandmother healing rock. Sparks of electricity jumped out of the rock into his hand hovering ten centimetres above. Such was the strength of reaction the tripod upon a which a camera was stationed was actually visibly vibrating. This was the day when the rocks began to share their narrative and legacy, and yes Karno's body was no longer present, but his spirit was there and instrumental in activating and opening up the rocks.

"Knock, Knock, Knocking on Heaven's Door"

Soon after the workshop the Culture Centre was legally taken from the Ramindjeri. Right now it serves no purpose in discussing the immorality, deceit and injustice in this theft and eviction beyond stating what those in control did was a cultural outrage and insult of the highest possible order. No-one has a justifiable explanation as to why this happened, but we have no doubt that the agreed positioning of the sacred rocks was a contributing factor. Once the eviction took place, the rocks no longer had a collective home, and that uncertainty left all our plans in a state of suspension with no light at the end of the tunnel.

I had nothing, and assumed all hope was lost in regards to displaying the rocks in formation on Ramindjeri land. So committed were we to this goal none of us had a Plan B, except Karno.

I woke one morning and for reasons unknown I decided to walk over to the curtains and pull them back. I had never done so before, but today it seemed like a good idea. And there perched on the roof but with its head bent leaning towards me, was a huge wedge-tailed eagle. I think most people would assume that upon pulling the curtains back the eagle was too close for comfort and would fly away. Not this one, not this time, it just kept staring directly at me. And as it did my mind was overwhelmed with one thought, the rocks must go on Ramindjeri tribal land, nowhere else would suffice, it just had to be there or nowhere else. Granted we had no location now, but that was irrelevant, the message was clear and simple that in the future the offer of a place would come to pass. Which, by the way, did take place a few years later and the location offered was on Ramindjeri land.

From that appearance of Karno in his totem spirit form until now, I have held fast to this feathered messenger from on high's guarantee.

There was One, Then Four, Three Soon After and Then - One Again

Never for a second did I expect Karno would appear in his totem form of the eagle when I was on country with two Original Elders examining the complete skeleton of a no-forehead Alien being at a burial site. I spent two days at different sites with a party of nearly twenty volunteers, the first day was at the burial site and the second was spent at three Original sites relatively close by.

Undeniably the archaeological highlight was examining the being that was neither a sapien nor hominid, but the spiritual blessing at the end of proceedings was no less intense or memorable. We gathered at the car park near a series of rock formations that looked decidedly artificial, our two days had come to a close and we were preparing to leave the site, when directly above us I first saw one wedge-tailed eagle circling.

I just knew instantly from first sighting that the eagle was Karno and told the others. None disagreed and what then followed only reinforced my claim of his temporary custodianship, within a minute three other eagles joined the first eagle as they continued circling directly above. Not long after the eagle I identified as being Karno, peeled off to the west, and the others followed evenly spaced in a single file. Then the leading eagle flew direct upwards, above the clouds and seemed to disappear, but about one minute later it descended and returned to the position above us. It then circled one last time then made its way towards the single file.

Undeniably many may claim there is no empirical proof Karno was involved and moreover, Karno was human and these carnivorous birds are not. Correct on both counts, but since Karno's passing, we have had eagle signs around our property of such quantity and quality that this appearance merely fits into an established pattern.

And Then There was One

As amazing and spectacular as these Karno feats were, they still are as a colleague of his, Wirritjin (Wirritjin is the name Karno gave to Stephen Robinson), put it, merely "party tricks." It was always more about what Karno said than did. His knowledge of Old Way Original culture and lore was unsurpassed and literally priceless.

Photo Description: Stephen Robinson (who Karno gave the name of "Wirritjin" and addressed Stephen that way)

But this isn't all about the past, his main focus was on what was coming, and in particular, how his doctrine of Wirritjin could be applied in future days.

Right now, we have lost our Dreaming, and it has been replaced with a nightmare of reality shows, fear in the streets and between the sheets. And every day the content gets worse.

It is time to start a new conversation, not with the politicians, cartels and those who manufacture the news bulletins, but with yourself. In doing so use a language that empowers the soul and planet. The Spirit/Soul language Frederic Slater and Karno W. understood is both the solution and our salvation. Karno is real, so is the First Language, everything else is secondary at best and more than likely a permanent distraction.

And then there was one, it is either Karno's way or no way, and we all get to choose, but it's all or nothing this time around, as there is no second choice.

Chapter Two:

A Friend of Karno: Natural Historian and Conservationist - Chris Thomson

You never know who is going to drop by whenever you are visiting Aunty Meryl at Trunkeena (in the Coorong). A close and dear friend of Karno, Chris dropped by to say hi to Aunty Meryl and Aunty Christine just before Christmas of 2022.

Photo Description: Chris Thompson at Trunkeena

David, from the Wirritjin Peggera:lin project was also visiting Trunkeena at the time and was lucky enough to get permission from Chris to record a short video interview for YouTube. When helping Steve Strong gather material for this book, Aunty Christine chose to also add the transcription of this video for this book.

Due to limitations imposed on him by his employer, Chris cannot reveal the type of work he does. But what we can say is that Chris works in the field of Natural History and Conservation, an area also very close to Karnos' heart. As you can imagine they became very close friends because of this mutual interest. Chris was also lucky enough to experience some of the spirit of the land that only an Original First Nations Elder can teach. And he touches on those spiritual experiences as well as how he first met Karno in this short, but powerful video which you are now also reading the transcription of in this book.

My name is Chris, and I have known Peter and Meryl for a very long time, Peter and Meryl introduced me to Karno at Trunkeena (Chris's home which is twelve clicks south near Magrath Flat called Tulatji), and they all used to come and visit here.

Photo Description: Karno with Uncle Peter Mansfield-Cameron and Peter's son Ravelle

Karno would always, when he came around, show interested in what we had at our place, because I had all these different Ngatji's (Aboriginal Totems) of animals, even crocodiles (which don't exist in the southern area of Australia where the Coorong is, they can only be found in the northern part of Australia), and we used to talk about that sort of stuff. The one thing that Karno was excited about was our large Southern Right Whale bone and the huge stuffed Wedge Tail Eagle, I think that was because Ramindjeri where Whale Law people and Karno's ngatji was the Wedge Tail Eagle.

Because of Karno's cultural interest in the eagle and whale bone we found through conversation that we had a bond through our environmental ideas and preservation. I've been involved in conservation most of my life and that natural history part of it became a bond straight away with Karno.

My fondest memory of Karno is his eyes I suppose more than anything, the way he used to look and just being able to pick up when he was going to be around (visiting the Coorong).

Peter and Meryl used to say that Karno was associated with the Wedge Tailed Eagle (this is Karno's Ngatji Totem), and nine times out of ten, I would see a Wedge Tailed Eagle outside of my bedroom window overlooking the Coorong because I lived right on the Coorong there and sure enough Karno was in the Coorong visiting Peter and Meryl.

The other thing that really struck me was the opportunity to go to Kangaroo Island on Karno's property there at Murray Lagoon the Mum:mo:wee (Gathering of the tribes held by Karno and the Ramindjeri people on Ramindjeri Country) and just the way they had it set-up and sitting in what I didn't realise was the way that the stocks were positioned around the fire. I felt like I was sitting inside a whale here and they all clicked on and said "yeah, yeah, that's where we are".

We did different walks around the place there and Karno was talking to me and the other people and explaining how the young Aboriginal people had to sit down and observe what was going on around them and to be aware of their surroundings, this was one of the cultural teachings that fostered a sense of belonging to country.

Being a white fella not picking things up (culturally) as quickly as what I should have, when we were walking around, he held the boomerang that he made, and we then sat down he was tapping the boomerang a little bit and explaining to the people how to sit there, watch country and the animals, and stuff like that. I was asking Karno more questions and he was getting a little frustrated with me. Karno asked me one particular question, but I was not sure what the question was about, and I just couldn't offer any answer and he whacked his boomerang down on to the ground so hard that it broke.

Boy oh boy, I really shit myself and thinking oh gee he is angry, what is going to happen here. But yeah, it all worked out good in the end. I was sick at the time at the Mum:mo:wee, there was bad spirits there and he took me aside and blew some smoke (cleansing ceremony performed with a coolamon) and talked about a few things. After this smoking ceremony I felt a lot better and got right back into enjoying the rest of the Mum:mo:wee.

And yes, he was just a magical man, and I am sorry he has passed on and I can't see him some more.

Chapter Three:

Christine & Meryl - Christine Walker & Meryl Mansfield

Photo Description: Meryl and Christine at Meryl's home called "Trunkeena".

Photo Description: Meryl Mansfield-Cameron teaching Karno cultural weaving.

First up let me introduce the man, he is a direct descendant of King Kondoy who was the leader of the Ramindjeri people.

His daughter Kalinga, which is her Ramindjeri name, is also known as Princess Kon, Sally, and Sarah. She had two sons, George and Joseph, who were both born on Kangaroo Island.

Joseph Walker is Karno's Great, Great Grandfather.

Stephen Walker is Joseph's son. Karno's Great Grandfather.

Charlie Henry Edward Walker, Karno's Grandfather, is Stephen Walker's son.

Lyndon Lancelot Walker is Karno's father.

Karno also has two sons, Joshua and Tyson. They are both strong, proud Ramindjeri warriors.

I first met Karno at a musical function at the Hilton Hotel, Burbridge Road Hilton. Karno was doing security at the function and said hello to Christine as she walked past. She said hello back and continued back to her seat. Karno went and spoke to George another guard and said he will marry the lady to whom he had just spoken to. Amazing, but George still recalls that comment to this day, even though Karno did not know who Christine was at the time. Two weeks later they both were again at the Hilton. They danced together for the whole evening. Christine commented how safe and secure she felt with Karno. This was wonderful as she had just divorced a highly abusive person. After enjoying each other's company for a few weeks, they decided that they would proceed slowly as Karno had also just ended a turbulent relationship.

After a period of two years Karno asked Christine if she would like to move in with him. She agreed and Karno was over the moon about it. From then on, they were inseparable.

Photo Description: Christine and Karno at their home "Wulde Waiirri" on Kangaroo Island (Karta)

Photo Description: Signpost for Karno and Christine's home on Kangaroo island "Wulde Waiirri"

At the time Karno had his own security company which blossomed after Christine came on board and did the admin side and allowed Karno to do what he excelled at. He was all about teaching and leading anyone who was interested in learning. There was a lot of employment for the company, through footy carnivals, cabarets, and almost every Aboriginal function. Unfortunately, there was a bit of a drop off after Karno openly supported the truth re Hindmarsh Island Bridge saga and those who didn't tried to blacklist his company which did not work in the long run, as Karno was happy to work for European folk which the other Aboriginal groups did not like. Karno was not racist like them. He was all about Wirritjin in action, he actually breathed lived it every day of his life.

During that time Karno was approached by the Sydney Olympic Committee requesting that his company oversee and organise the security at the games. This being a fine example of Wirritjin, Karno agreed.

The requirements of his company were to check for snipers and bombs etc. a very important role which required excellent observation and vigilance. After being addressed by the army bosses one boss pointed to Karno and asked him to explain in his own words what the address meant.

Karno replied with a smirk "search and destroy sir," the guy looked back at Karno laughing and said, "I want you on my team" This was yet another practical example Karno's humor once again breaking the ice.

After six weeks at the Olympics, they returned to Adelaide and then went to Alice Springs to the Yiperinya Music Festival. Took a team of 20 staff and worked alongside the Shane Ryde Security Company. Shane was so chuffed to be working with Karno that he just handed the reins to him. Once that task was completed Karno's team returned to work at Hindmarsh Bridge for a further two months.

For many years to come Karno continued his security work along with teaching and sharing the skills and philosophy involved in martial arts. He taught a different style which incorporated all different styles from around the world combined with the Ramindjeri style. This style of Martial Arts was called Ramindjeri Martial Arts which was also the name of Karno's Dojo (school).

Martial Arts was a huge part of Karno's life. Teaching and sharing knowledge with other Martial Arts school was a great way to learn a variety of styles, this was his biggest joy, carrying out his spiritually driven duty to pass on the knowledge his spirits of the Old's imparted into his soul substance. His magnetism and charisma drew those that were eager to learn. Karno was in his element doing Weaponry and other styles. He extracted qualities and skill from people who were unaware that they had such gifts, mentally and physically. He pushed me to the max, he wanted me to be the best i could be in order to bury the submission that I had been subjected to in a previous abusive relationship.

This proved to be very successful, because if challenged one could change to a style that the opponent was not trained in. Whether engaged in free-sparring or something more threatening nobody ever got the better of Karno. So many young men completely turned their lifestyle around for the better after this training. They gained self-belief and discipline. So all-encompassing yet distinctly Ramindjeri this unique form of martial arts was accepted by the Australian Martial Arts Association. Not all schools are accepted into that Association which in itself was a great recommendation and achievement.

Photo Description: Karno flanked on either side by two Martial Arts students

Karno was the Chairperson of Black Deaths in Custody, working closely alongside him where Alice Dixon and Charlotte Walker. Karno's role was to identify the deceased as well as being a court representative and counsellor to connected family members. Around this time Karno and Michael Mansell travelled to Belgium, France and London and they were the first people to return from overseas with Aboriginal remains. They both got a huge shock while in Belgium discovering that children in schools were being taught that Aboriginals were extinct in Australia. The students in Belgium were very quickly convinced by Karno that this was not correct, "that's lies what they are teaching you in school, that's lies" Karno repeated. While in London at Trafalgar Square Karno spoke to a huge crowd enlightening them why he and Mansell were there. His speech lasted approximately one hour, after which he answered many questions which were put to him.

On their arrival back at Sydney Airport they were confronted by TV cameras with bright lights which impaired Karno's vision. At the same time someone tried to touch the remains to which Karno reacted defensively to protect them by punching the person who caused such a great offence to culture and protocol. Karno was arrested but was later released and no charges were laid.

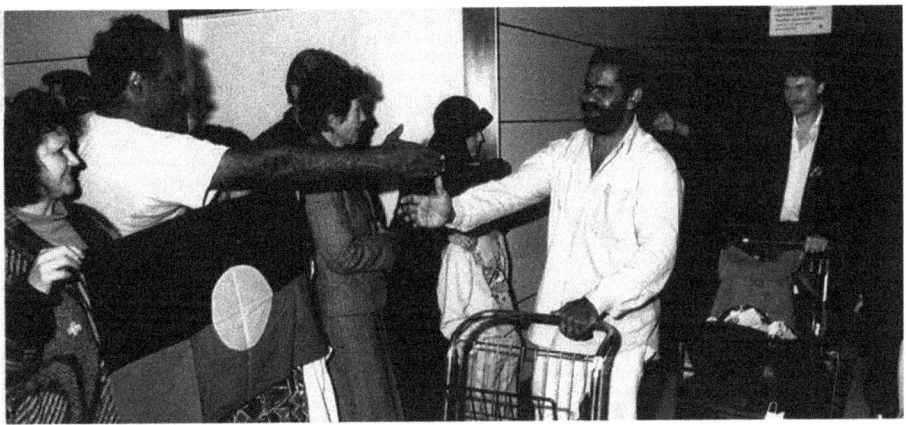

Photo Description: Karno and Michael Mansell being welcomed at Sydney Airport in the early 90's

Karno and Christine continued with their security work along with martial art classes and also lodged a native title claim to prove that the Ramindjeri were a nation unto themselves. It was also proven that prior to settlement their northern boundary was the Torrens River and that the Kaurna is a post-colonial group whose original country was north of the Torrens. The Ramindjeri claim was never rejected and still recognised by the State Heritage to this day. In addition to that his subsequent groundbreaking claim for sovereignty was never overturned.

Photo Description: Karno, Dr Irene Watson and Mark McMurtrie, leader of the Original Tribal Sovereign Federation.

Karno and some of his main support group throughout Native Title saga pictured above is Karno with Dr Irene Watson and Mark McMurtrie.

His most encouraging supporter was Judge Justice Mansfield who strongly encouraged Karno not to give up but to keep going and he himself respected Karno's knowledge of cultural boundary prior to settlement, and to get the truth out there.

Photo Description: Karno holding Wedge-tailed Eagle feather.

As life continued forward relatives, Peter and Meryl Mansfield-Cameron, were always asking older folk if they knew the whereabouts of Charlie Walker. He was an older brother of Peter's mum Harriet Dorothy (Dot) Mansfield nee Walker who was keen to find him. One day whilst at Raukkan Peter was cutting grass when an old gentleman approached Peter and said hello. Meryl asked him if he knew Charlie and was thrilled to hear that he did. He told her that Charlie was his sister Vida's father-in-law and that she had married Lancelot Walker who was Charlie's son. Their son Karno was well known and highly respected by many.

At around the same time Karno was at TAFE and while there got chatting to a fellow student (Susan Hand) who told him that her nanna was Edith Walker Charlie's sister. Karno went and met her mum Patricia Hand who gave him the Mansfields phone number. He called them and each family were very keen to meet. Well talk about a great catch up. Each family were hearing stories about relatives they didn't know about, and a strong bond was formed between them all, spending time with each other at every opportunity.

Peter Mansfield-Cameron and Karno had a spiritual connection which no words could describe, each having different spiritual powers which worked together perfectly. That bond was so amazing to witness. While being asked to go to St Helens Catholic school as there were remains exposed during the construction of a new playground. Karno and Peter went the to have a look along with the Kaurna men and anthropologist Colin Pardotte. They returned to where they were staying and ate dinner. After that chatting outside Peter said they must be careful as there is another skeleton about one metre away. Christine asked him how he could say that as only one skeleton had been exposed. He said he didn't know how or why, but he knew he was right and went on to describe his vision. He said it was a young male with a cracked skull and angry, so be careful when you uncover him (and he was there). As Peter said this, a strong gust of wind came from the exact spot the warrior was interred, causing Bluey Roberts to be very unsteady on his feet and knocking Kaurna man Joseph Mitchell to the ground (Joe never returned to that job). Everyone was stunned at Peter's accurate description.

Karno also told the Kaurna guys lots of cultural stories relating to the area. These Kaurna guys commented that they had learned more about culture in the past few days than ever before and loved it. Colin the anthropologist agreed stating that he would love to have Peter and Karno present at all times wherever and whenever he was on country. There were too many stories to relate about similar incidences, but they are etched in the memories of those who witnessed them.

THE MOVE TO KANGAROO ISLAND

After many months of negotiation, the L.G. Walker Family Trust gained the lease of a property on Kangaroo Island (Karta) from ILC (Indigenous Land Council) to be used for cultural education etc. The Walker family have very strong links to the area as their Great grandfather Joseph Walker and his brother George Walker were born there in the 1830s. Their mother Kalinga (fullblood) was the daughter of the Head man of the Ramindjeri KONDOY, King Kondoy as he was called by white people.

There is much recorded history re; Kondoy and Kalinga who were the first people to practise Wirritjin.

After settling in Karno and Christine held many cultural gatherings along with schools and colleges coming frequently to stay for cultural education requirements. They all loved Karno's very demonstrative way of teaching. Karno could read the land and the stories in it and could keep an audience captivated. He was also involved with KI Tourism doing what he loved doing, teaching people about Ramindjeri culture.

The property they named Wulde Waiirri (Eagle Heaven), Eagle representing Karno's Ngartji (totem) and Waiirri means Heaven. Other Tribal groups call KI the land of the dead, which is not correct. Ngurunderi told people after they passed away to follow him across KI to the western most point, plunge into the sea, cleanse themselves and then follow him to Waiirri Heaven or Wairriiwar home among the stars.

AN AWARD RECEIVED

There was a time when Karno was doing security in the Port Adelaide Mall at a time when there was a high crime rate. Karno and his team were called to a meeting by Chief Inspector Bruce James Martin in regard to working out strategies to curb the crime rate. Following this meeting Karno and his team took over, working in a combined effort with Port Adelaide Enfield Council and police. The outcome was very good resulting in a big reduction in the crime rate.

Karno had his own way of dealing with this matter, which we call KUNGKUNGULLUN (loving and caring). He did not arrest them but talked to them about changing their way of seeing things and then organised transport home. Karno and his team only left to knock off after the whole area (Port Adelaide CBD) was quiet. The crime rate dropped by 75%, a fantastic outcome for which Karno received a big award and was officially recognised as CITIZEN OF THE YEAR.

His people skills were amazing.

Chapter Four:

A YOUNG MAN'S CAMP AT WULDE WAIIRRI - Nick Leidig

A group of young men from Adelaide came to Wulde Waiirri (Kangaroo island) under the guidance of Nick Leidig and Robert Champion, the group was named Kurruru. The very first words Karno said to them was "welcome boys, one thing I will tell you all straight up, is that without question you will do as you are told." The boys thrived on what they were being taught and shown while camping on country (ruwe) the whole time. They were doing their own thing in the mornings and then were walking on country with Karno and Uncle Peter Mansfield-Cameron in the afternoons absorbing culture, loving it and learning heaps.

Photo Description: Uncle Peter Mansfield-Cameron and Karno with camp bus behind them.

On completion they were given a certificate of achievement and asked to write a comment about Karno and Uncle Peter. One lad said he couldn't think of something to say about Uncle Peter, as he doesn't say much, Peter right behind him replied "but I know what you are thinking mate." The lad's face lit up and he had no problems writing a comment down. Karno thrived on teaching young and old, even though at times he knew they were not absorbing it for the correct reasons. Some (nephews included) would pick up a bit here and there, later using it to make them look like men of knowledge. Karno would say, "they are not the chosen ones."

The young men from the camp say it turned their lives around and sent us a calendar with current pictures of themselves. All had successful careers, we were so proud of them. AFL footballers, actors, pilots and so on. One lady asked Karno what had they done to her grandson, he came back a different young man.

An Evening of Magic

During a visit to Trunkeena on the Coorong (Peter and Meryl Mansfields home) Karno and Peter were discussing the fact that a prominent Aboriginal group were breaking protocol big time. They felt it would be right to ask the spirits of Elders passed if they could help get things back on track somehow. They decided to ask that night feeling it was the right time as it was a full moon. The full moon (Makari Mimini) represents a pregnant woman ready to drop (give birth), which is a good time for people to let go of their problems by asking the spirits if they could help. Peter handed Karno a kanaki (wadi) which belonged to his great Grandfather Mileraoun who is the head man of the Milmeindjera Lakalindjeri (clan).

They went and sat on the edge of the veranda side shoulder to shoulder, talking to the spirits. Karno stopped and said, "Uncle I can't stop the thing turning in my hand" Peter said not to worry keep asking, which they did. The wives were sitting behind them and also asking. Christine told Meryl to look between the men, there was smoke coming from their sides which rose up between them and narrowed above their heads like a chimney. Meryl said Peter might be smoking and was told promptly by him that he wasn't. All continued to ask for honesty and truth to prevail and thanked the spirits for listening. Not long after that night word had spread that Kudatji man had been jumping loudly on the roof of Camp Coorong terrifying everyone inside and letting them know that they were doing the wrong thing. Karno and Christine also heard the same thing on Kangaroo Island. Things certainly improved after that evening.

Chapter Five:

Christine - Christine Walker

Leader:

Whilst Karno didn't really class himself as a leader, but he was very aware others did. His way of life was I guess in a leadership role, in the way of always expecting truth, honesty, integrity and above all respect for your fellow man.

He had standards that he kept whether that was in the role of security, or martial arts teachings, or everyday life, and he expected all the above in return.

He also had a strong passion for music and in his younger days he approached his Aunty Leila Rankine to add an Electric Instrument section to the Centre for Aboriginal Studies in Music. Karno then enrolled with CASM and started his own band called the Muttaruks. This Electric Instrument Curriculum he helped to inspire was responsible for generating many other students who then went on to form some of Australia's most influential bands of the 80's. For example, bands such as, No Fixed Address, Coloured Stone and Us Mob. His influence on the music industry was celebrated in the Adelaide Festival Theatres first ever Mural by artist Carol Ruff, called "Aboriginals discovered Captain Cook"

Photo Description: The first ever mural painted on the side of Adelaide's iconic festival theatre, painted by Carol Ruff and includes Karno playing bass guitar as a young man.

Photo Description: Inset of above Mural featuring Karno playing Bass Guitar

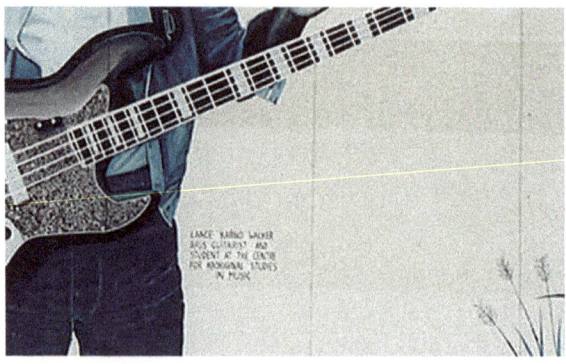

Photo Description: Zoomed in version of above inset showing Karno's using Karno' birthname of Lance "Karno" Walker

Photo Description: Karno playing Guitar on the Verandah of his home at Wulde Waiirri.

He was there for family and friends alike. Not just a great leader but also a person you could go to in times, when in of need for a listening ear or to help you solve a problem. Everything rolled into one which made him a great leader someone who you could depend upon and look up to.

Loreman:

His teachings were of culture, language, stories of learning, dreaming and land (ruwe). He passed on his teachings from childhood to adulthood, everything and some more. He was in his glory teaching and storytelling, whether it was around the fire or around the kitchen table, he oozed confidence and felt that we should all know our cultural history no matter where you come from. A very proud Ramindjeri man.

Karno never ever looked at himself as an Elder or Loreman but knew he made a difference in a lot of the young fellows' lives. He said you don't have to be the eldest nor the youngest to be an Elder, he was the chosen one and he held that role in high regard, and with honour.

Visionary:

Vision is hard to explain, and he followed his MIWI (gut feeling) most of the time. Whether that was about people or just about something about to happen.

Karno also was on a mission for Ramindjeri people to have the right to speak on and for their own country and for the Ramindjeri to be recognized as true custodians of their country, that was his main reason for going to Native Title Court.

He envisioned a Ramindjeri Cultural Centre and drew it on paper, for his people to have somewhere of their own to display their crafts, artefacts and history.

"Spirit knows no colour" he always said, "as above so below" was another saying that was central to his teachings. He treated everyone the same, his reason for doing security was because he wanted to be there for his people to help break down barriers and stop so many being arrested for nothing, which did happen a lot. I have seen this happen myself. Ramindjeri people were well known as "Peacemakers and Law Enforcers" and Karno getting together a security team made him satisfied he was still carrying that tradition on.

One of Karno's greatest visions is "Wirritjin;Peggera:lin" (Blackfella /Whitefella working/coming together as one) he/we lived it every day. He also taught this fundamental mantra in his Ramindjeri Martial Arts" lessons and practiced it whilst we were working security. It is and will always be an ongoing practice.

Chapter Six:

Unbulara - Unbulara

King Condoy was the Ramindjeri Whale Loreman. He was the leader of the Ramindjeri Nation which was made up of approximately fourteen clans. Matthew Flinders and Nicolas Baudin concluded the mapping of South Australia at Encounter Bay in about 1802. This is Ramindjeri country and the Ramindjeri people were known to be friendly and are documented as the peace makers and law enforcers.

King Condoy's daughter Kalinga known as Sally/Sarah in Aboriginal lore married William Walker. Sally and William had two sons, George and Joseph. Joseph Walker was born on Kangaroo Island in about 1836 and died on the 13th of May 1931 aged 95. He was the 2nd son of William and Sally. He married Emily from Salt Creek, Coorong Nation Tanganikald. She was born most probably during 1852 and died on the 6th of February 1907. They had a family of six children. Their sixth children and youngest son, Joseph Walker Junior obtained land on the Coorong. Joseph Walker's son Stephen Walker who was born on the 19th of July 1883 and died on the 2nd of August 1939 aged 63.

He is buried at Meningie and was the first son of Joseph and Emily. Stephen married twice. His first wife was Eliza Elizabeth Davis who was born in Keith. They married on the 9th of February 1902 when Stephen was aged 27 years and Eliza was aged 18 years. They had seven children; the eldest son Charles Henry Edward Walker was Karno's grandfather. Stephen and his second wife Amy Cameron born on the 31st of October 1888 at Point McLeary, had two children, Alfred Joseph Walker and Harriett Dorothy Jean Walker. Harriett Dorothy Jean Walker, who was my mother, was born on the 15th of February 1928 at George Wright's house on the Coorong.

Karno Walker Loreman, deadly warrior, teacher, leader, healer and Elder lived his Culture every day and believed in the Old Ways, respect, culture and passing knowledge to the others and especially the young.

Karno did not just share knowledge, Lore and protocol. He was also passionate about Wirritjin and the ongoing difficulties our people face in today's Australia. Deaths in Custody being one of these unresolved issues, as he felt it to be a deed of duty in order to get this right through the path of honesty and truth.

In the photo (pictured right) is Karno speaking about deaths in custody to a group in Adelaide on the steps of Parliament House.

We had many spiritual gatherings and Wulde Waiirri on Kangaroo Island (Ramindjeri name Karta meaning island). At one particular gathering, which was attended by Graham Hancock and his wife Santha, we had a fire, not the sacred fire used for Mum:mo:wee, as this meeting was more personalised. We were all sitting around the fire, having a good yarn, then Karno magically appeared out of nowhere standing in front of the fire, did a welcome to country in both original language and English. It was at this place and time that Karno gave me my Ramindjeri skin name "Unbulara," which is the Ramindjeri word for "little whirl wind", then all of sudden Karno disappeared. Within seconds he reappeared next to his wife Christine on the opposite side of the fire.

When Karno reappeared, he was dressed the same as he was before, he had his Kangaroo skin on and had his face markings painted on. We all went quiet, each of us wondering how he did this, and how could he just disappear and moments later appear like this. The truth was he is a Magic Man. I was one of ten people who were witness to this real magic and none of us had any doubt it was real, and that Karno was a very special human being.

Karno had many talents not just the ability to disappear and reappear, but also to know what someone was doing, even those hundreds of kilometres away. He also knew just when and what knowledge to give a person on their Cultural knowledge journey.

Karno was and always will be remembered as an honourable, truthful and culturally knowledgeable man. Karno constantly said, "spirit knows no colour," and lived his life sharing Culture with all who wanted to learn.

Karno was teaching me and making me stand up as a Ramindjeri Elder in times where sharing our story was important, even though I felt I was not quite sure if I was ready. He obviously knew I was. I remember one time we were in Victor Harbor walking toward the Museum, a group of young students and their teachers came out of the Museum. Immediately Karno and Christine started speaking to them, Christine introduced Karno and myself as the Ramindjeri Elders of the area and when Karno finished his talk, he turned to me and said it's your turn Aunt. So, I did as he said, and I actually felt confident and capable of doing so. He knew I would be, even if at first, I did not.

Karno also told me I had to do the women's dance ceremony leading others on the site where the skeletal remains we found during excavation of the Southern Expressway, the remains were now ready for repatriation and needed the correct ceremonies before being removed. This was another time where Karno knew I was able to do something I did not know I could do. I did this and realised Karno knew best, as he always did.

At the Mum:mo:wee gatherings Karno made me do more and more. At the last gathering Karno was at, as he and I were sitting on the grass having a little chat he said to me "Aunt you need to do more." Karno had shown me the Cultural sites on Karta, he walked with me around the property and surrounds telling the Dreamtime stories of the Ramindjeri, the story of Marni (how the Goanna got its claws/talons) and the Wururi story about how the Ramindjeri spoke the first language. Karno felt comfortable with his teaching of the knowledge he shared with me, which is what I needed to know to become more involved.

I now have the knowledge and confidence to stand up at gatherings when talking with others about my Culture and Lore. I owe my knowledge and confidence to Karno and Christine Walker, they both taught me, gave me confidence, and made me stand up when they knew I was ready.

Photo Description: Unbulara, Mark McMurtrie and Karno studying the OSTF Kangaroo skin treaty document that Karno and Unbulara cosigned on behalf of the Ramindjeri. This document was introduced as evidence during Karno's Sovereignty case.

Karno will always be missed by all who knew him. There has never been nor will there ever be another Elder like Karno Walker, now, or during these recent times, he gave so much knowledge, and he was so giving of his time to help others and to share his culture with all. Karno always said, "it's not proper, should be old ways". Karno Walker had so much cultural knowledge, spirituality, skills that amazed and stunned people and a great sense of humour. I also remember times laughing and talking with Karno and Christine.

Karno had a special way of teaching me sometimes telling me and sometimes giving me a cryptic question to work out for myself. I will always be grateful to Karno, teaching me a lot about how much information to give and when someone should think about it for themselves.

I know there are many people who Karno touched in a special way. There were so many people he shared knowledge and culture with, and none doubted his ability to be a presence like no other. Karno was a very special person, and I believe that so many times, even now, Karno is leading me and guiding me.

Karno will never be forgotten by all who knew him or knew of him.

Chapter Seven:

Walking with Karno Walker - Darren McElroy

My journey and adventures with Karno Walker begin at the studios of Bay FM community radio Byron Bay. As the producer and presenter of the Cultural awareness show I received an interview request from a local author and archaeologist named Steven Strong. While researching for the interview I came across some of Steven's research that involved a Dreaming story talking about "little people", further researching revealed a deep knowledge of Aboriginal culture and lore. Shortly after the interview with Steven I called my family in Adelaide South Australia to explain I've just interviewed Steven Strong, and he is researching Dreaming stories about "Little People". My family instructed me to bring Steven down to Adelaide to meet with members of the Ramindjeri.

Photo Description: Darren McElroy aka DJ Terra Nullus behind the mixing desk at Bay FM during the broadcast of his weekly show "Wirritjin" a show about "Blackfella – Whitefella Dreaming: DJ Terra Nullus presents a programme of Indigenous music, culture, news and special events."

I arranged and organised for Steven and myself to travel to Adelaide. The timing for the visit was perfect because the Ramindjeri were commissioned to repatriate buried ancestors to make way for a rail corridor. Steven and I had the opportunity to meet Uncles, Aunties and cousins of the Ramindjeri along with extended family members. This meeting was a pivotal time for the both of us, setting us on our perspective paths.

Following this meeting Steven and Karno formed a bond, sharing information around cultural archaeology that grew over time, leading to a number of collaborations and projects together. The first gathering was around the discovery of a Standing Stones site in Northern New South Wales. This site required some interpretation that Steve and Karno worked on together, eventuating in Karno being invited to the area by the Minjungbal and Arakwal Bumberlin custodians of the site. Harry Boyd, Jarmbi Githabul and other Original Elders welcomed Karno to the area and site. To enter the site a small group entered first led by Harry & Karno. To announce their welcome, Karno called on the hawks (a totem of the area), and as the story goes the hawks started to circle over the site, firstly 3 hawks, then 5 and finally eight, circled directly above Karno while singing them up, this story was conveyed to me by two members of the group, truly outstanding.

As Karno and Steven's collaboration grew, we became involved with a visiting international celebrity, Graham Hancock, a novelist of human antiquity, consciousness, science and archaeology, famous for writing the 'Fingerprints of the Gods'. It turned out that Graham had been following Steven's research, leading to Steven and myself being tasked with flying to Adelaide with a small entourage to collect Graham and take him to meet with Karno on Kangaroo Island.

On the ferry over to Kangaroo island Graham's anticipation was growing on what to expect. Travelling from the ferry to 'Wulde Waiirri' on Kangaroo Island we became lost in a heavy mist, when we finally got reception to ring Karno, we were directed to the site.

Karno shared sacred sites, Dreaming stories and on one special night around the fire when Aunty Unbulara received her tribal name, Karno appeared painted up, holding a spear and a boomerang, stepping backwards out of the glow of the fire and then completely disappearing, then re-appearing on the opposite side of the fire like magic to the astonishment of everyone around the fire.

My name is Darren McElroy, a descendant of the Ramindjeri and Karno came into my life at a time when I was looking for cultural knowledge and belonging to bolster my faith giving me the strength to identify with my Aboriginal ancestry, something that had been eluding me for many years.

Spending time with Karno was some of the most magical and informative times of my life. I wish I could have spent more time learning from Karno.

Photo Description: Darren McElroy in his background with a wild butterfly that flew onto his hand to pose for this photo.

Chapter Eight:

Working With Karno - Nick Leidig

My name is Nick Leidig, I am a nephew to Uncle Karno, My lineage is : King Kondoy, Leader of the Ramindjeri. Kalinga (Ramindjeri name), also known as Princess Kon, Sally or Sarah, Kondoy's daughter married William Walker sealer/whaler. George Walker, Kalinga's eldest son born on K.I. Reuben Walker, was the son of George.

Photo Description: Nick Leidig addresses a group of people while proudly wearing his official Ramindjeri shirt.

Arthur Thomas Walker married Mabel Pantoni, Arthur was killed in action in WW1. (Myself and the committee are honouring his life in the Warrior Spirit section of the Wirritjin Peggera:lin project's website.)

Anzac Walker son of Reuben, Arthur married Linda Giles. Linda Walker nee: Leidig, my mother.

I would like to say that I had a lot of encounters with Uncle Karno over the years, catch ups etc. None however was as everlasting and rewarding as the youth camp on Kangaroo Island. I, like Uncle Karno, am a proud Ramindjeri Man.

So, it goes back about 10-13 years ago when I was working at Kurruru Indigenous Youth Performing Arts, and we ran a boy's program and Uncle Karno took a great interest in supporting young Aboriginal boys at risk.

Unfortunately, during this time there was the whole "gang of 49" media furore at the time sensationalizing a whole range of issues going on with young Aboriginal males at the time and Uncle Karno was a fantastic mentor and I was there with others as well, which we will not mention in this account. But they were offering young Aboriginal boys ways out of their situation, instead of resorting to crime which often led onto going back into the juvenile detention system or resorting to any sort of violence.

So, Uncle Karno, through Ramindjeri culture, invited me as I was sort of the program officer at the time. I met with the mentors of the program and organized for a group of young Aboriginal boys to come over to Kangaroo Island.

So, he (Uncle Karno) invited us over to the Ramindjeri place (Wulde Waiirri) on Kangaroo Island near Murray Lagoon and we met Karno, Auntie Christine and another Ramindjeri Elder who has since passed away, Uncle Peter Mansfield-Cameron. They hosted us for three or four nights, of this group, probably the youngest was 10 and the oldest was about 16 or 17. We set up our tents and camped on the property sleeping under the stars.

Uncle Karno taught them Ramindjeri culture and the program actually was called Binnanendi boys' youth program–"Binnanendi," which is a Kaurna word meaning "journey into manhood" and you couldn't have hoped for a better Aboriginal cultural leader and mentor than Uncle Karno to help guide these young Aboriginal males through their journey into manhood. But there was so much more he shared with us, Karno was also guiding and teaching them Ramindjeri culture, around the fire at night, and around the property and took us to significant places around the island during the day.

So that was roughly what the Old Way program was about and there is footage, a lot of video footage too I just mentioned that was filmed by a young Aboriginal male on the last day in the shed of Wulde Waiirri. At the time he basically took all the video footage then we got and another guy to edit it and put it all together.

But yeah, it was really fantastic that this young Aboriginal male said, "look I want to take on that responsibility." His name was Clayton, and he did a great job.

Photo Description: A group photo of Kurruru Youth Camp students at Wulde Waiirri.

My Fondest Memory of the of the Camp

I think when you're dealing with young Aboriginal boys who don't have many positive role models in their life and they come up to you and during the camp and afterwards at the camp and they speak about the positive experiences they had in their interactions with Uncle Karno, that, from my perspective it is as good as it gets.

Probably the fondest memory I have of Uncle Karno is actually when we rocked up to Kangaroo Island and as everyone knows who has been there, you go over on the ferry and as we dock and the ferry sort of drops the door or gate or whatever you want to call it and the cars and trucks come off the ferry. Then, as we all started to walk out of the ferry after all the vehicles were coming off, there was Uncle Karno painted up in his traditional paint and traditional clothing and I thought I was looking like a statue. He just stood still and watched everyone, and you could see the tourists were like looking at this guy like they were astounded and taking photos and everything and he just stood there with such pride and was there to welcome not just us but everyone. He was welcoming all of us onto Kangaroo Island. Even though he wasn't at all disrespectful to the tourists, he only focused on us, and it just felt like he was there to make us feel welcome and for all the young males to feel like Uncle Karno is here to look after us and welcome us to Kangaroo Island. I think with all of us our jaws hit the ground when we saw him, and it wasn't expected at all. He (Uncle Karno) went and did this off his own back and yeah, that was my fondest memory.

Now I'll tell you we've heard many welcomes to countries and all have been important, but that was one incredible welcome to Country. I wish I took a photo and maybe if only Christine allowed me to, I would have included it in the video, but no one expected it. Not a welcome like that, yeah so that's my fondest memory.

The Positive Long-Term Effect this Youth Camp had on the Male Youths who Attended

I still know the kids who sat with Karno and some of them I'm still in regular contact with, there was two of those kids who ended up in the AFL (Australian Football League) and it could have even been three, but these are the same kids who everyone thought were just going to end up in juvenile detention. So, it was amazing and there are digital stories about program run by Karno which we have put up on the Wirritjin Peggera:lin website.

Chapter Nine:

SHARING CULTURE in the BUSH - Peggy Rismiller O.A.M. (Katerai:peri) & Mike McKelvey O.A.M. (Nguridji)

Pelican Lagoon Kangaroo Island, Australia

Karno spent a lot of time in the mallee woodlands of Karta. He liked working and sharing experiences with Katerai:peri (Peggy), Nguridji (Mike) and their many international volunteers.

Photo Description: Karno with Peggy Rismiller and her partner Mike McKelvey

Photo Description: Mike McKelvey and Karno holding the "Talking Stick"

Photo Description: Karno addressing conservation volunteers

On one occasion we brought two books to Karno, a high school Chemistry text and a high school Physics book. Karno said "I was raised in Culture. I was taught to hear and listen, to look and see. I learned to read the world around me, listen to it speak. Today many people learn from books like these two. In the front of this Chemistry book is the Periodic Chart of the Elements. For me the elements are nature's alphabet. The elements form compounds, compounds are nature's words. Physics is nature's grammar. Sometimes it is hard for people to hear or see nature. Nature becomes a resource to be used, a product to be acquired, something to consume, a momentary escape and distraction from their day-to-day lifestyle. With natures language I read the land like an encyclopedia. This is a gateway to the universe."

Time and people have passed, culture and stories live on. Today Karnos' Wirritjin Peggera:lin is shared around the world, from generation to generation. "Wirritjin is a Ramindjeri word. It means Black Fella White Fella coming together in peace. Peggera:lin is sacred Dreaming. Wirritjin Peggera:lin is a way of Life.*"

*Karno Walker, Wulde Waiirri Mum:mo:wee, Karta 2015 Katerai:peri and Nguridji, Karta 2015, Muwerang Mum:mo:wee

Chapter Ten:

Spirit knows No Colour - Peggy Rismiller O.A.M., Mike McKelvey O.A.M. & Richard Bell

Several times a year Karno would meet a group of young people at their school's bush campus along the North Coast of Kangaroo Island. These young folk came from all around the world, their families from a wide range of social and economic situations.

Photo Description for above and below photos: Karno with Scotch College Teacher Richard Bell and his students.

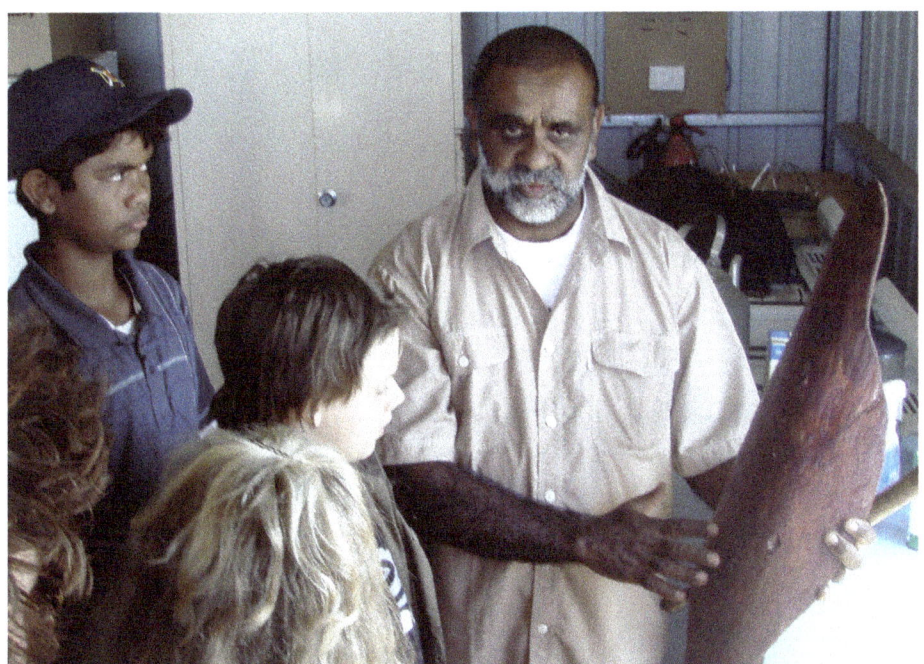

The days were often cool. The young folk gathered down wind of the Sugar Gum fire enjoying its gentle heat. Karno and his Island Elders stood facing the young folk with backs toward the sea. There were often pods of dolphin and Southern Right Whales dotting the passage, the off- shore islands and land stretching towards the Great Australian Bight. This area was strong in nature and Culture.

Karno would welcome everyone to Country in the Ramindjeri language and again in their common language, English. He would add a coolamon of Blue Bush to the glowing coals. The rich smoke would drift across everyone. He would say "Spirit knows no colour."

These were days with many new experiences, days of new friendships and exploring values in nature's classroom.

Chapter Eleven:

Planting Circles - Peggy Rismiller O.A.M.

Erosion and salt scars were spreading across Kangaroo Island. Long before the Australian Government decided to plant a million trees, community groups were working to heal the land. There were special days where neighbours came together to plant native tube stock. It was contagious work, others volunteered to help. Word spread along the bush telegraph and city folk joined winter planting festivals.

At the time we worked with international groups of volunteers. Karno joined these groups sharing his humour and Culture. He would show how to plant the tender seedlings with respect, always having the sun on your back, so its energy went through you and into the young plant.

Photo Description: Karno relaxing around the fire at the end of the day with conservation volunteers at Pelican Lagoon.

We would start early, and he would sometimes begin the day by sharing The Red Kangaroo Dawn Dreaming story. At the end of the day, we would watch the evening stars and he would share the Dreaming of Marni, the Goanna born into a different world.

Plantings were chosen to help address erosion and soil health. Sometimes special salt tolerant plants were chosen to help shift soil chemistry and prepare the way for future plant successions. Karno shared his understanding of chemistry and how these plants and the microorganisms that thrived along with them were the power houses for healthy landscapes.

Karno did not plant in rows or straight lines. He used nature as his model. "Look how the bush bends and twist. See how that adds strength to the growing plants. Mix the plants. Let the different kinds of plant share their energy and outcomes with others. Help build strong, healthy communities." Sometimes he would talk about gatherings, folk coming together from all the directions. "People would come together in great circles. Today tree circles still grow across the land. They are living reminders of our ancestors, of how to live."

Photo Description: Sacred Fire at Wulde Waiirri

Photo Description: Karno and Mike

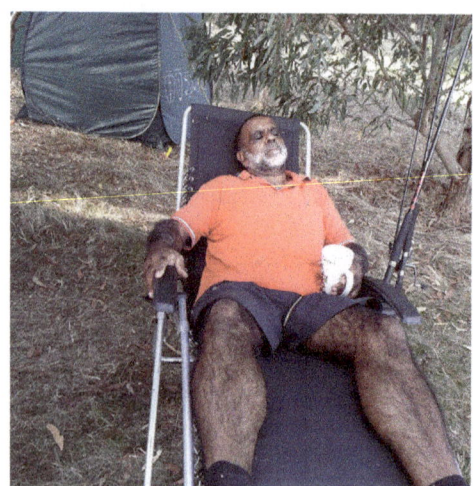

Chapter Twelve:

In Memoria: The Teachings and Supervision Style of Karno Walker
Who am I ? - Dr Christine Gillies

My name is Christine Gillies, and I was honoured to be Karno's cousin. Our familial bond was not a coincidence but a testament to our shared ancestry. We both traced our lineage back to the same apical ancestors on the Walker side of the family: Emily Yriandinyeri, a Tanganekald woman from Salt Creek, and her husband, Joseph Walker, born in 1836 on the Karta [1] of Kangaroo Island. William, the son of Kalinga, daughter of King Kondoy of the Ramindjeri lakinyeri, and William Walker – a sealer, a boat builder, and an interisland trader, were pivotal figures in our lineage, connecting us in a profound and enduring way.

Kalinga, our esteemed ancestors, played pivotal roles in history. She was a member of the first pre-colonisation contact party and a crucial aid provider to the occupants of the first South Australian settler ship. These settlers arrived on KI half-starved and very unwell. A year later, in improved health, they left KI for a short journey to the mainland and disembarked at Glenelg to impose the Dominion of South Australia. However, it is disheartening that Kalinga and William's descendants did not receive the same kindness from the settler's descendants, a stark contrast to their significant contributions to the early history of South Australia.

My lineage followed Stephen Walker, connecting us to individuals bearing the surnames Walker, Cameron, and Mansfield Cameron. Conversely, those with surnames like Koolmatrie and Trevorrow descended from Stephen and Charlie's sisters or cousins, namely Charlotte, Rachel, Emily, and Alice.

Despite our shared heritage, Karno and I had different upbringings that reflected our family's geographical and cultural diversity. I grew up in Naracoorte, a town built over the shared keinari [2] but still individual lands of the Meintangk, Marditjali and Potaruwutj peoples. On the other hand, Karno's childhood was spent at Point McLeay Mission, now Raukkan Aboriginal Reserve, Brinkley Aboriginal Reserve or Murrungoon, which was not a managed mission, and further up the river with his sister. These diverse upbringings enriched our understanding of our family's history and heritage, fostering a deep appreciation for our shared roots.

We both shared a close bond with our respective grandparents, a bond that was nurtured by our shared heritage. To the best of my knowledge, which is sometimes patchy, Stephen Walker's children were never residents of Point McLeay Mission. Still, they visited whilst in the care of Amy Cameron-Walker as she was the non-resident cook at the Point McLeay Mission Hospital. This was a short while after the early death in childbirth of their mother, Eliza Elizabeth Davies of Keith. Ellen and her siblings were then raised by the Davis family in what is now the oldest Settler Cottage in South Australia at Keith, then by Amy Cameron-Walker, Stephen's second wife and then by Ellen's and Karno's grandfather's older sister, Aunty May Loydd, in Meningie South Australia. These grandparents played a significant role in shaping our understanding of our family's history and heritage.

First Meeting

I first encountered Karno during my childhood, likely at Brinkley Aboriginal Reserve in East Wellington [3]. It was a typical Christmas school holiday, and my brother and I stayed with our grandmother -Ellen Walker-Gillies. With our aunties of the same age in Darwin visiting their sister, Nanna visited some relatives I had not met before. This visit marked my introduction to an Aboriginal reserve, and I was old enough to be deeply affected by the sight of people living in what others despairingly refer to as "humpies" with compressed dirt floors in parts of the buildings and no hot water. Initially, I was apprehensive, but my fear dissipated as I witnessed the warmth and hospitality of the relatives within, particularly towards my grandmother, whom they loved and were so excited to see. They were also keen to quiz me closely and liked that I listened intently to the family stories they told.

Photo Description: Group photo with Karno as a child highlighted within circle.

Amidst the gathering and endless cups of tea and storytelling, a little younger boy, Karno, entered the scene, exuding cheeky smiles and jests. His presence brought a light-heartedness to the gathering. Karno soon insisted we join him for a swim, leading us to the water's edge, where a tree with a rope swing awaited. He gleefully swung into the water, attempting somersaults and swimming—just the thing in the hot weather of January.

Karno showed us around, including where he slept and kept his belongings. I remember innocently inquiring, "Where are your books?" I was raised to believe that books were essential and reading necessary. It worried me that he did not appear to have his books to read. However, we all had a beautiful day. We laughed until our sides ached, drank endless tea, and ate several batches of scones, and as we left, I remember someone calling out, "Come back soon". I was happy to meet these lovely new relatives, looked forward to returning, and said we will. However, that was never to occur!

Each time I returned to my grandmothers for holidays, I would ask when we would visit the relatives on the river [or lagoon] again. I would pack spare already-read books for my cousin without a library in anticipation. Always a little headstrong, I demanded to know why we were not returning and to give me the address so others could take me. My grandmother told me they were good people, the best, but I must not tell other people about them or that we visited them at home. I was angry and said, "That's wrong." She agreed it was wrong but said that if people knew we were related and visited, they would treat me differently. I persisted. In the end, Nanna became angry with me, a rare occurrence. She said, "Look, Chris, we can't change it! Let it go, and don't make trouble for others by telling people. They are our secret! You have no idea what trouble you can bring on other children and people if you say too much, and government services will find out about us." So, I kept quiet but was not too fond of it! However, I grew up in a large extended family; other relatives came to Nanna's house, and we went to Meningie, Murray Bridge, visiting relatives and Port Elliot swimming.

Reconnection

I am trained as a Clinical Psychologist. In about 2006, I was asked if I would be prepared to help establish an Indigenous Association within the Australian Psychological Society to begin implementing the then-draft version of the United Nations Declaration of Indigenous Peoples Human Rights into the professional practice of psychologists. I agreed.

At subsequent meetings in Perth and Melbourne, I heard of the psychologist Joyleen Koolmatrie and met Elizabeth Cameron Traub, and I realised we or their husbands were probably related. I remember my grandmother talking about relatives with the same name and visiting them when I was young. I decided to search for the family I had met decades before. I contacted Uncle Tom Trevorrow and Uncle Neville Gollan, seniors, who knew exactly who I was and provided information, particularly about my great-grandfather, Stephen Walker. Uncle Tom Trevorrow, whose grandmother Alice was a Walker, suggested I contact Karno Walker, Chairman of the Ramindjeri Heritage Association and gave me his telephone number.

When I first made telephone contact with Karno, he and his partner, Christine, were living on Kangaroo Island and were very busy. Karno was surprised that I had also lived on KI in the past. Karno immediately made time to speak to me for lengthy periods, which continued regularly over the next two years. I was immediately comfortable with him and could hear my long-since deceased lovely grandmother's sense of humour and laugh in his way of joking. It was comforting. It took me a little while to realise that he was the shiny boy I had known many years before, and I was so happy to have finally reconnected.

I soon realised how smart he was and noticed that he could decipher meaning simultaneously at multiple levels without any trouble. I realised that he had extensive knowledge of laws related to Indigenous people and had an excellent memory. I was impressed that he and Christine, with other relatives, knew so much of the family history and traditional culture passed on from Karno's grandfather, the Murrungoon Elders, the Mansfield-Cameron's extensive Family records and Yaralidi cultural understanding, and Christine's tireless research and support to help Karno with his work. I had seen so many others struggling to find a single forebear, so it seemed incredible that the family history was well documented and supported by Mansfield-Cameron's photo collection that imaged family members right back to the turn of the last century.

I soon realised that Karno and I shared a love of history that has developed in many family members. We both liked to find the underlying cause of anomalies and ferret out the answers to questions with no known answer. I also recognise that Karno was good at surrounding himself with people with good research skills and legal knowledge. However, as I expected and had worried over the years, Karno's childhood education was of a poor standard. Still, he had the backbone to take himself off to TAFE in his early 20s for literacy training and, to my surprise, was now an avid reader of every historical text about the Ramindjeri he could lay his hands on. It turned out he had managed without my extra reading library! He also appeared to have excellent motivational and organisational skills. Gatherings were organised on KI. I also noticed that he would not compromise and continue working in a way he thought was wrong or unethical, which appears to be a family trait. He also devoted hundreds and hundreds of hours on an ongoing basis to helping others reconnect culturally and get on the right path.

I would telephone Karno from NSW on Sundays. We would speak for lengthy periods. He was determined that I should learn suitable elements for a female of Ramindjeri Lore and the traditional stories relevant to our family. He repeatedly told me the Ramindjeri story of Wururi the Spider. He was keen that I understood that the first to eat the flesh of the spider and gain intelligible speech was the Ramindjeri. In other words, they were recorded in traditional storytelling as the first clans to have language.

A facility with language was certainly evident in the story of Kalinga, who learnt English and French from sealers before colonisation and was fluent in several Aboriginal languages. Kalinga's linguistic skills were much appreciated by early explorers of the area and are well documented in historical records. She also provided the Ramindjeri Language to German Missionaries to record.

Cultural Supervision

Eventually, I asked Karno to provide "Cultural Supervision" regarding topics I grappled with in psychological work. Karno advised me to incorporate the principles that came to us by word of mouth from one generation to the next, from "true people of country," from manuscripts about cultural practice written by members of the Walker family early last century [4], from old letters and documents and from the advice given by members of the Walker family when acting as informants for anthropologists or German missionaries and information from the Mansfield-Cameron records. He encouraged me to resist the contamination of the cultural understanding the English missionaries introduced during the religious conversion and the contamination of clan-based knowledge occurring in modern land rights processes.

This approach did not always lead to the same conclusions that other researchers had reported after the consultation of an Indigenous advisory group. We would often consider the conclusions of published findings, and Karno would explain why he disagreed with them. Karno devoted many hours to discussing issues related to this topic with me, sharing his experiences and observations from related projects. He wanted me to understand why different consultations can produce different results. Eventually, I asked him how to ensure one consults with the right people for each issue of interest.

What is Inclusive Consulting?

Karno emphasised that variability exists in the cultural knowledge recommended by Indigenous people, both within consultation groups from the same area and between different clan groups. He highlighted that people from the same location may have acquired cultural understanding via diverse cultural transmission processes affecting the advice given. This difference, he said, was inadequately delineated in consultation reports. He said that one group does not speak for another and that consulting only one group will lead to a distorted or shallow finding. We realised that the knowledge base developed without considering this variability in the knowledge transmission process would unlikely to inform accurate predictive research and assessment methods.

The cultural transmission processes Karno identified were:

1. Advisors whose cultural knowledge includes missionary corruption and suppressed traditional information.

2. Advisors who rely on ancestral knowledge passed down orally through family elders regarding practices in a specific clan territory.

3. Advisors engaged in Aboriginal language, clan boundary, place name recovery, cultural

restoration, and truth-telling efforts; and

4. Advisors who adhere to cultural understanding based on the post-Mabo land rights framework. This framework establishes "Indigenous Nations" for land rights administration purposes. It incorporates all clan areas that shared mythical figures in their creation stories and had family members who had been herded into an off-country central mission. This approach was designed to accommodate those disconnected from their original clan country due to multigenerational enforced missionisation, disconnection to some or all related families, disconnection to original clan lands and customs and prohibitions on cultural practice. However, nation boundaries will cross language groups and clan lands and potentially include individuals traditionally prevented from communicating. Consequently, there's no unified cultural practice except those agreed upon after the post-missionary era. Healing knowledge from this group may also be contaminated by psychological healing theory and research practice in local medical services. This construct may lead to an enlarged territory managed by a Native title management group, potentially providing financial incentives for claims managers. However, the approach also aligns with government agendas that seek to disconnect Indigenous people from their traditional clan lands. It also allows the implementation of a Western Administrative Management model, replacing the traditional Aboriginal Land Connection model. This approach contradicts the conventional focus on land, language, and people maintained by those who retain their original clan connections and customs and pursue a clan-based pathway to cultural recovery.

Under guidelines established to unpack the United Nations Declaration on the Rights of Indigenous Peoples, modern government policies mandate "inclusive consulting" of Indigenous people in all Indigenous research endeavours. While many research reports claim to have conducted inclusive consulting, the term "inclusive" is often not precisely defined, and descriptions of how the consulting was supposed to be inclusive are not provided.

My discussions with Karno suggest that genuine inclusivity in consulting is only achieved if all group representatives contribute. Each group has the right to autonomous consultation, and research reports should adequately define the cultural transmission pathway of its consultants. Failure to consult each group in institutional research suggests the consultation was: 1. Not genuinely inclusive. 2. Failed to implement Australia's international human rights obligations, which are implemented on the ground by its social and educational institutions, and 3. Contravened Departmental Research Policy, which claims they will always provide "inclusive consultation".

We discussed many other topics, including broadening the relevant variable template in Aboriginal Forensic Assessment and risk assessment tools. I introduced tools and assessment issues, drawing on my experience conducting evaluations, and he made suggestions based on his experience as Chair of the S.A. Aboriginal Death in Custody Committee, running the South Australian Aboriginal Security Team (S.A.A.S.T), and his uncontaminated cultural knowledge. We would also consider deidentified case examples and issues, such as Aboriginal-specific requirements to assess motive, truthfulness, contributing factors, and strategies to deter repeat offenders.

Karno's insights were precious, as crime levels significantly decreased when he and his partner provided an Aboriginal security service. Secondary to the security work, he had implemented successful interventions to guide youth from involvement in the criminal justice system. He employed martial arts and self-control teachings that he developed called "Streetwise", which utilised traditional stick training. Tools like the traditional Kanaki were used to practise defence skills if attacked. Instructions were given in the Ramindjeri language. The Karta names were also drawn from the Ramindjeri language. This helped young ones learn their traditional language and defence skills. This exemplifies Karno's desire to imbed youth into the old language, self-defence, and an attitude of keeping out of trouble and controlling aggression. He was a born teacher directed by the spirits of the Elders! He seized every opportunity and process to impart cultural knowledge to anyone willing to listen.

Another example of his approach was how Karno conveyed to young people the significance of the S.A. Police Emblem for guiding correct behaviour. The emblem includes the wattle plant, a Ngatji protector plant for the clans of the Ramindjeri. He said the presence of the wattle plant signified the need for youth cooperation and respect toward law enforcement if undergoing a police force check or during any other contact. Confrontation and aggression, he said, were not helpful. We agreed it only increases the risk of multiple charges, introduced distortions in the rate of progression through the risk classification assessment system, leading to a greater likelihood of imprisonment and showed a lack of respect for Aboriginal Lore.

Our discussions also delved into Aboriginal astronomy, where I learned from Karno about the Ramindjeri being renowned and respected by central Australian clans for their astronomical prowess, earning them the title "Keepers of the Stars." Karno also illuminated how other Ngatji protector symbols or elements, like thunder and lightning, were also intertwined with celestial phenomena. He encouraged me to travel to see rock carvings depicting these astronomical observations. He was also astounded that I had studied one subject of astronomy at university and been involved in supporting the development of a planetarium. He laughed and said -it's in the blood and later included the idea of a planetarium in his plan for a Ramindjeri Heritage Centre.

During such discussions, Karno also helped me understand that my Nanna had no alternative when she would not let me talk about the existence of my relatives from Murrungoon, including Karno. She had to protect me and other grandchildren. She particularly had to defend my father's younger sisters, who were still minors and the same age as me, from the Aboriginal child removal system. This was even more heavily impressed upon me when I understood that they and I were cousins to the only Aboriginal person to be compensated as a member of the stolen generation in Australia. Bruce Lampard–Trevorrow won a case in the SA Supreme Court for being falsely imprisoned in the name of child protection. Bruce was not the first and, unfortunately, not the last! Reading the court transcripts from the case in the SA Supreme Court made us question who exactly required protection from whom! We also thought Kalinga and William's descendants deserved better and were appalled that many of the procedures that destroyed Bruce's life are still in use today.

Furthermore, Karno elucidated his rationale for advocating for the return of Indigenous governance structures when he was a party member, which included the King of Tahiti, making representations to the United Nations in Geneva calling for "The Return of the Kings". He highlighted the historical falsehoods perpetuated by colonising nations that claimed no governance structures existed pre-settlement and that the existing population would benefit from the imposition of the English administration system. Karno cited examples along the South Australian Coast: Indigenous leaders like King Condoy at Cape Jervis, King Peter of the Yaraldi, and, down as far as Kingston, Queen Ethel Watson. Each used governance processes, exemplary conduct, and communication skills to preserve adherence to cultural law. Each was an example of a headman or woman, but named kings and queens by the settlers, indicating the settlers knew that a governance structure existed, and which head person was in charge. Karno wanted to dispute the foundational assumption that made settlement lawful in the eyes of British Law and call for more significant Indigenous self-rule under the leadership of Indigenous head men and women.

Photo Description: Karno and Mark McMurtrie with the King of Tahiti at the United Nations in Geneva Switzerland.

Photo Description: Mark McMurtrie (OSTF Leader) with Karno listening on as Mark addresses the United Nations.

Ramindjeri men take concerns to UN forum

In July, Ramindjeri law man and spokesman Karno Walker and Mark Koolmatrie, attended the third and final seminar in the United Nations Treaty Series, in Switzerland.

The seminar was conducted by the UN's Office of the High Commissioner for Human Rights. The topic of discussion being "Strengthening Partnership between Indigenous Peoples and States: treaties, agreements and other constructive arrangements".

The event was held at the Palais des Nations in Geneva, Switzerland.

During the two days, Mr Walker and Mr Koolmatrie, with Original Sovereign Tribal Federation convenor Mark McMurtrie, told the UN about the legal anomalies facing the UN nation state of Australia.

"Namely, that the Sovereign on this land isn't the Queen, it is the Tribes and their people who are the legal and lawful Sovereigns," Mr Walker said.

The paper delivered by the three was read into the record at the end of the seminar, and shocked a number of those who heard the information it held, Mr Walker said. A paper by Tanganekald Meintangk elder Dr Irene Watson was also accepted for consideration at the forum.

"The UN was informed that various tribes on this continent had also already requested the Crown's representatives to decolonise their lands, but the Australian state had not complied.

"We also indicated that we will approach the relevant station within the UN to obtain an undertaking from the UN that it will demand compliance by its member state to our demands," Mr Walker said.

"We believe we have gotten our message across to a certain degree, but to what practical degree that is will be determined by the belligerence of the state (Australia) in respect of its playing by the rules of the international community and finally showing respect to the tribes here," he said.

"We hope the UN is as quick to respond to the concerns of the ethnic cleansing of the indigenous people of this continent as they are in Afghanistan or Iraq.

"We voiced our concerns, for example, that UNESCO, a part of the UN, is sponsoring the reconstruction of the Buddhas of Banyami in Afghanistan, yet the UN and others sit silently while mining interests desecrate our art, treasures and culture - which are tens of thousands of years older and at least equally socially, culturally and spiritually valuable," Mr Walker said.

Karno also shared insights into the efforts of the Ramindjeri Heritage Association to establish Ramindjeri as a distinct native title group, separate from the Ngarrindjeri and Kaurna claims. The first claim had been submitted, and the court accepted all information provided but called for additional information. This was provided. His Honour, Judge Mansfield, found the claim needed to be referred to the then-highest Australian court - the Privy Council in England. His Honour could not rule because ruling on Ramindjeri Sovereignty was beyond his jurisdiction or terms of reference, such as the uniqueness of material contained in the claim. His Honour also told Karno not to give up or give in and to keep going. He understood Karno was interested in obtaining the truth -not power or monetary gain and that the claim included unique information that may challenge prior judgements. Karno's reason for applying for Native title in the first place was for Ramindjeri recognition and the rights of Ramindjeri people to speak on behalf of their land.

In our conversations, I also asked Karno to consider the Social and Emotional Well-being model used by Indigenous psychologists and its relationship to Closing the Gap. By context, immediately after the UN and then the World Health Organisation was formed after WW 2, it began providing new regular directives to its member states about the health and wellbeing service infrastructure it needed to implement to start raising the health, well-being, and longevity of the entire population.

Over the past 70 years, all UN signatories have been required to implement each WHO sitting's recommendation via legislation and directives to their relevant departments. The implementation of these directives has progressively and incrementally raised the standard of health and well-being of mainstream Western populations through education, housing, and welfare, including in Australia.

Unfortunately, in the settler colonies, including Australia, the infrastructure established for the mainstream population, regardless of location, occurred at a very different rate to those established for Aboriginal reserves, missions and later communities.

The difference in life expectancy seen today reflects the increases in life expectancy for those who received the infrastructure development in childhood and later over the past 70 years, compared to the lower life expectancy for those who did not!

Karno had an uncle who was killed in WW1 and cousins who served in both WW1 and WW2. Still, tragically, Karno was denied access to post-war health infrastructure development that is known to lengthen life expectancy while living on Aboriginal reserves and missions and, predictably, years later, became one of the statistics for sudden premature death that is known to result from withheld support for long term health.

I still remember that bright, shiny boy swinging across the water, full of the possibilities to do anything in life, and the enormous personal effort he exerted to catch up on his denied educational skills, helping others, mentoring others, preserving the teachings of the true people of the country and the truthtellers of his childhood, being an excellent partner, preventing deaths in custody, and helping youth not to fall into the criminal justice trap.

I wanted to help Karno with books as a child, but he ultimately helped me. It was not fair, and I don't forget it. I fervently believe that if I could see that the people on the reserve, including Karno, needed extra resources as a primary school-aged child, I also don't believe those who withheld the necessary resources to build longevity were blind to the outcome they were engineering. The predictable outcome had already been fully outlined by the UN and WHO.

That leaves a bitter taste!
He deserved better!

Nunki mica

Dr Christine Gillies
UOW Wollongong

Footnotes

1. Karta – A Ramindjeri word meaning any island

2. Keinari – A Meintangk word meaning boundary

3. Brinkley Aboriginal Reserve or Murrungoon – The reserve known by the Aboriginal clans as Murrungoon holds a significant place in Aboriginal history as the home of Aboriginals who remained steadfast in their traditional culture and wished to live in freedom. They resisted the altered version of Aboriginal mythical stories and administration imposed by English missionaries. These stories also contained crucial mapping information for navigating the River Murray, imparted ethical training, and conveyed terms regarding the traditional Aboriginal administrative system. Missionaries, aiming for Christian conversion and undermining traditional ways, distorted these narratives and imposed them on the residents of the mission. Those at Murrungoon, refusing to succumb to this cultural erasure, demanded independence from the mission and its teachings. Despite being entitled to the same support as any Australian of their time, they did not receive it, nor did they even receive the meagre support given at Raukkan Aboriginal Reserve. This group, the original truthtellers, must not be forgotten! Karno followed them and was committed to truth-telling. The Murrungoon residents departed the mission and settled near East Wellington, rejecting the hypocritical teachings that were clear: claiming truth-telling as a divine commandment while employing deceptive techniques learned from Missionary School that were anything but truthful and clear to those strong in culture, who were also required to be truthful on cultural grounds. Reverend Taplin played a vital role in distorting Aboriginal traditions. He reimagined Ngurunderi, the mythic "Land shape changer" who journeyed down the Murray River following Pondi the cod, as a Christian creator figure. Knowledge of the traditional creators was suppressed. Additionally, he renamed the yanarumi "tendi" and distorted how problem-solving and discussion occurred under the chairmanship of the clever man or munkumboli before he gave a final judgement. The term munkumboli, was renamed "Rupelle. " The munkumboli possessed insight and democratic management skills and could model appropriate behaviour and provide a trusted final judgement with wisdom. The word Rupelle was also the name of a mischievous and bad spirit from Mt Gambier that was used by Aboriginal parents to caution their children. Parents would say don't go near the water - Rupelle, the bad spirit will get you! The method of adopting the same term as a bad spirit for the munkumboli surreptitiously co-opted Aboriginal parents into transmitting a negative perception of Aboriginal leadership and traditional, peaceful, and respectful problem-solving and lawfulness while trying to keep their children safe from drowning. I hope they are happy with their handy work!

4. The Reuben Walker Manuscript – in Norman Tindale, (1934-7) 2 Journal of Researches in the South East of South Australia. Adelaide, Anthropology Archive, South Australian Museum.

* Karno's name is used with the permission of his partner.

Chapter Thirteen:

In Conversation (Part 1) - Colin Watego & Steven Strong

The next two chapters were not written but spoken. Colin chose not to write a response but talk about his dealings and understandings in relation to Karno. There are two sections in his response and were given on different days. A few questions were repeated, but because his replies were not the same but more extensions, we decided to leave the general format unedited.

Conversation No. 1

Steve: Tell us about the first time you ever met Karno Walker.

Colin: All right, mate. Well, before I do, what I would love to do is just acknowledge the traditional custodians of where you and I are on at the moment. Of the Elders past, present and emerging, and also pay respect to Ramindjeri Elders and Karno's ancestors as well as our ancestors from our other countries. But also, mate, I want to reach out further in acknowledging the ancestry of those that come from other countries whose origins started somewhere else in the world and now call Australia home.

Now going back to uh when I first met Uncle Karno it was quite an interesting day. I had been, during that time, in full-time uniform for quite a long time. So, a little bit of background first, my name is Col Watego I'm a proud Bundjalung, a proud Torres Strait Islander of South Sea Islander descent and spent many years in the Australian Defence Force, forty-three years plus, actually. At the time I met Karno, I was the Australian Defence Force Senior Indigenous Recruitment Officer. We first met in at a military ceremony in Adelaide on the Torrens Parade Ground at the unveiling of two magnificent bronze statues, one a male and the other a female, and they were of Aboriginal descent.

This was an extremely important ceremony and among the dignitaries was the Governor General of Australia, Her Excellency, Quentin Bryce. Now in my role in uniform, was that I was very honoured and privileged to be able to lay a wreath at that ceremony on behalf of the Army. Now this is where it gets interesting as I had a very special seat right up the front but from that positioning, I couldn't see the two monuments. Now it just so happened at that time, one of our leaders from Canberra was attending and due to an administrative error was no seat for him.

So, what happened was that I offered up my seat and I went to the back of the podium and waited there until I was called to come to lay the wreath after the statues were unveiled.

And it was there and then standing at the back that I met Karno. I believe it was timely but also preplanned because had I not given up my seat, had I not for whatever reason, moved to the rear of the podium, I may not have had that opportunity to meet Karno. So there we were standing at the back together until I was then called to lay the wreath which

I placed at the base of the memorial, and then saluted.

What struck me as I did that was the facial features of the male soldier. It was almost like I was looking at my great uncle who died in Africa. It was just the most amazing experience. After the ceremony, Karno and I got together, and we also caught up with two Canadian Indigenous soldiers, and we've got a photograph of those guys.

Photo description: Uncle Karno and Uncle Colin Watego flanked by Canadian Indigenous Officers, the man next to Karno was currently serving, the men in the burgundy coats are wearing the uniform of Retired Native American Veterans.

We had a bit of a yarn, and we hit it off straight away, there was this very special relationship formed. I honestly believe from a spiritual perspective; we had a kindred spirit which we were to find out later how that actually developed. Ironically as time went on, we found that we both shared the same personal totem, the eagle.

Past that first meeting, we caught up with each other on several occasions later, but at that particular time, there was just something very special about the way and place we met.

After everyone left, I went back to the memorial and just spent a little bit of time there in the presence of those magnificent bronze statues that represented so many things for our people, our cultures, our families, our kinship, our ceremonies, but first and foremost it was about sacrifice. I think that was the biggest thing that come out of that. For me it is the sacrifice of not just our soldiers who served, who went overseas, but all our peoples since Cook came sailing up the east coast of Australia.

That's where I first met Uncle Karno for the very first time.

Photo description: Karno and David Rathman

Steve: I remember the first time I met Karno, which was a different situation to your first meeting in some ways, yet in other ways so similar. It was when he was supervising the removal of skulls and bones from the Seaford Rail Extension and then he was putting them back into country giving ceremony before reburial. He literally reeked of Old Ways, and the look in his eyes the very first time he really focused on me, I still have trouble finding the words.

Can you think back to that time and tell me the first impact he had upon you when you're standing alongside him there at the back of the room? Is there anything that strikes you immediately when you first saw Karno, his presence, his demeanour, the way he spoke, something along those lines?

Colin: Absolutely. There was an aura and presence around Karno, you just knew deep down that you were standing alongside someone who had very, very high values. I think one of the things that resonated the two of us is that when I got to meet and know Karno better and when we got to share conversation time together in both formal and informal settings, there was this amazing respect that I had for him. To begin with I didn't know Karno's history and pedigree. I really didn't know who Karno was. I wasn't aware of the depth of his relationship with culture, country and community,

When you stand with him when you're doing ceremony and you're on sacred ground, you know where you are, you know what you're doing, you can feel his overwhelming connection, the spiritual energy pours out of him. I still remember like it was yesterday the two of us standing together, he wore a black suit. I can still see him standing there and me I'm in my uniform, I'm holding a wreath and he's standing there beside me, and it was almost like we were sharing mutual respect. Not only for those that we went to honour, but also for each other. You know what I mean?

Steve: Yes.

Colin: Which became more apparent later as we did journey together. You couldn't help but note that when you were with him there was a sense of respect and honour. You knew that you were standing next to someone who had very high ideals and values. Sometimes you don't even have to speak to know those things. He actually resonates that through his whole presence and everything he does.

Steve: What was his reason for being at that meeting. Did he mention to you why he was actually there?

Colin: No, not then, but I do believe I know why now. Karno comes from a family of warriors. One of his ancestors, Uncle Arthur Walker, served in World War One and I find that extremely interesting because so did my grandfather and two of my great uncles, my grandfather's oldest brother and my grandfather's brother-in-law, that's my grandmother's brother, and they were all over there at the same time together.

I can imagine that my grandfather and Uncle Arthur just bumping into each other somewhere along the track, you know what I mean? Like I intuitively felt like it had to have happened at some stage and that this is like a repeat of that further down the line, isn't it?

Irrespective of whether our ancestors did meet, Karno is special, he was a lore man. He was a visionary. One of the things I do know for certain was that he had tremendous respect for warriors and honouring warrior spirit. I found that out later through other ceremonies and at different times. But during that event, what was happening when the unveiling of those two statues took place, whoever attended, whoever was there, whoever was present or whoever supported that, had a very strong support for our First Nations men and women in World War Two who served in defending Australia.

We found a photograph the other day of Uncle Karno being introduced to her Excellency, Quentin Bryce, and it shows them shaking hands at the ceremony. It's all about respect, to the highest degree and this is not what I think, this is what I know.

Photo Description: Uncle Karno meeting her excellency the Governor General of Australia, Quentin Bryce.

Steve: One of the things you said is when you did ceremony, you learned about different aspects of Karno, where he was coming from. Did Karno Kano ever take you through an Old Way ceremony? I thought it'd be nice if you could explain how that actually happened for those people who don't quite get it.

Colin: I want to talk about Mum: mo: wee and totems as well, but let's start with ceremony. I've done some ceremonies with Karno. And to this day I can remember them basically point by point, and these days I don't remember a lot.

Steve: Can you remember one of the times he took you through ceremony and took you through culture?

Colin: Absolutely. In fact, I can remember every time. I had the absolute extreme honour of being part of a ceremony where Karno had presented to the then chief of the army a magnificent kangaroo skin with nine layers of Dreaming. Now, this happened at Muwerang/Kent Reserve Victor Harbour which was the last known camping ground of the Ramindjeri and it happened on the first of August, which is a very significant date because of the military history attached to this date. I do believe that everything happens at a time for a purpose. There are no accidents or coincidences in this event happening on the first of August. And I know because Uncle Karno and I, we spoke about dates and that date was selected specifically. If you go back through Australian history, you will find that on the first of August 1870 was when the British actually handed over colonization, to the colonial structure within each country and withdrew.

And it was the same day and date that we presented a magnificent kangaroo skin to the chief of army, Lieutenant General David Morrison A O, and this ceremony took place on sacred Ramindjeri grounds at Victor Harbor.

Photo Description: Uncle Karno and Lieutenant General David Morrison A O at Muwerang (Kent Reserve, Victor Harbor, South Australia) with the Kangaroo Skin Karno presented to him.

Photo Description: Sargent John Angel-Hand, Uncle Karno, Lieutenant General David Morrison A O and Warrant Officer 1 Colin Watego at Muwerang (Kent Reserve, Victor Harbor, South Australia) with the Kangaroo Skin Karno presented to him.

And I remember speaking at length acknowledging this repetition in timing, because I was the military person liaising between defence and Uncle Karno. The kangaroo skin has a series of totems, and you'll see an overlaying symbolism that is very significant. For example, you'll see the stars that make up the Southern Cross.

It's also on our national flag, and has become a beacon for our soldiers, sailors, airmen and air women. But it is more than that, it represents a beacon for the spiritual returning of the spirit of those who like Uncle Arthur who died on the battlefields. Also, what is equally significant is that there are two magnificent pictures of our Ramindjeri ancestors. It ensures that if someone like Uncle Arthur doesn't come home, their spirit is never lost but does return.

There is a serpent that starts at the base of the tail as it curves its way up towards the kangaroo's tail bone. And there are a series of totems right at the bottom. But the most significant figure on the skin is the Aboriginal warrior with his tools and his weaponry who is standing up straight, tall and very proud. And it sends a very clear message to our people, to all peoples, that we are proud people. We all need to look at that and view that through the lens of this is where you come from. This is who you are. You need to find your place or space in today's environment, which is very difficult and very challenging, but it has to be done.

I think that' the reasons why Karno and I got on so very well together is that we shared the same vision for our young people, for all our people making better choices, to make good choices which must lead on to a better future.

Getting back to the sacred artwork, near the tail there are three paths/totems to choose from, the sea turtle represents Navy, the goanna stands for the Army and the dragonfly which is the totem for the Air Force. What I feel is the central motif upon which everything else revolves is a magnificent picture of a World War One soldier who is positioned between two Australian totems of a kangaroo and emu. The kangaroo is on the left and the emu is on the right, their footprints which are black halfway up then turn a white colour up towards the top of the skin and is above these white footprints, is a depiction of the rising sun. The way I see it the juxtaposition of white and black footprints standing underneath the rising sun is all about Wirritjin.

Steve: That term is something Karno never let go, he was all about us all walking together. But I did want to come back another term and role you attributed to Karno, you said often he was a Loreman, and I fully agree with you. We both know what that means but there's a lot of people maybe reading this book that may not quite understand its true meaning. They might have this vision of something like a sheriff with a badge. Could you explain to people what an Old Way Loreman actually is?

Colin: OK, mate. Look, we're very blessed because there are many things that are passed down to our people to do journey and there are special people that are responsible to make sure that we do that journey properly. I guess if you wanted to bring it back to a white fella thinking, you could say he is a law man with a badge, but this is much deeper than this. With our lore men they are, they, first of all, highly regarded and respected members of community and they are responsible for ensuring that our ancestral practices continue.

And that's essentially what sustains our spirits and soul. You know, you look at history and for whatever reason you see that there are many cultures that are now extinct. For me personally, I have so much regard and respect for our knowledge holders, our Elders, but also for our Lore Men because it's through the passing down their really rich ceremonial practices that has sustained our people since the beginning. Even so, everyone will tell you they haven't had an easy ride, but above all the setbacks you got to remember, our people are very spiritual, that is our cultural base, and the Loremen are responsible for carrying on or passing down their guidance and knowledge of protocol and Old Ways. They are obliged to carry on those very necessary rich practices that we need to adhere to because they're based on the values that underpin of our existence. We've gotta keep coming back to the ultimate question, what do people value?

We hold a very, very, strong value and understanding in regards to our creation. Our Loremen make sure that, whether it's through our waterways, whether it's through our landforms, our vegetation or our animal life, there is this elemental appreciation that everything is bound and belongs together. That is why we all have totems, we learn everything from a perspective of don't take for the sake of taking, just take what you need. That way there's always something left for someone else, and that eternal truth is taught through our lore men, and it's passed on down through our Elders as well.

But unfortunately, with the loss of our culture, spiritual ceremonies, sacred sites and the land itself the lore keepers have become silent under this onslaught of neglect. All these values are very vital aspects of sustainability for our people which we need to reclaim. And that is one of the things I loved about Karno. He was happy to share that culture.

There's a quote from Karno that I'd like you to remember. There was something he said soon after we first met that really resonated with me, and I wrote it down straight away. He said that the lore meant that you must ensure that we journey. The Loreman/woman's role was to guide you while on that journey.

Steve: Well, I think that's a brilliant quote, I've never heard it said that way, but I think that sums up why we are here. And I want to follow that observation of cause and effect up with two more questions. I want to go back to when you spoke about your shared animal totem. You said that both yourself and Karno shared the same totem, which is the eagle.

Now, some people might say, well, that's interesting, but how does that come about Colin? How does this happen? I saw him do things with eagles that left me speechless. I stood there with my mouth open. I couldn't believe what I was witnessing and watching. How does such a miraculous partnership come about?

Colin: Like I said before, to begin with I didn't know that the eagle was his totem and Karno didn't know that the eagle was my personal totem either. Now, let me just say, you need to have a little bit of understanding about totems first.

In a general sense, totems are really important in our culture, because it's through totems and skin our birthright and connections are established. Because, well back in the day before the British came, they never had birth certificates, so you had to be very careful when you when you wanted to meet someone and maybe you to start up a relationship with someone that was too closely linked through genes or blood ties. Though they might have been separated and they didn't know each other their kinship and their totems were unsuitable for this to happen, and because of this any relationship of that personal level was forbidden. In the old days such knowledge was mandatory knowledge the young ones were taught early on.

Separate to that there's also a personal totem that people identify with, and I guess for me, mine goes back to childhood actually, right back. Don't ask me how, why or whatever, but I can remember as a very young person for whatever reason, always having a very strong affiliation with water and of course with the eagle. And you wouldn't read about it. I have still got my football jersey after all these years when I played for the Eagles at Mount Gravatt.

Up in Yolngu country when they do the Garma Festival, I remember sharing the story with Aunty Christine, they were doing the final dance when all the tribes were coming together at the farewell ceremony and fair dinkum, I looked up and there was this magnificent eagle just kept hovering over and around the event. There are certain times where, like I said, I don't believe things happen by accident. There have been so many times where I've been somewhere or doing something and I just look up and see the eagle. Of course, the eagle means something to me personally from myself, but when I see the eagle now, I don't just think of the eagle as my totem, I think of it also as Karno's totem as well.

Steve: Can I add another dimension to that by asking you a question that flows out of the non-Original society and their science that places humans on a pyramid above all other animals. So, when we talk about totems and their power and status what is the difference between the soul of an eagle and your soul?

Colin: That's a really, really good question. For me personally, I guess I'm very blessed because you see not only do I love my culture, practice my culture I also have very strong faith and the eagle plays a role in that as well-it's like a partnership of equals. I personally resonate with that when you talk about the soul, my totem the eagle is my equal. Same goes for every other totem that others have, we all share the same spirit, our Creator is the source of all souls, human, dolphin, tree, deep down we are all same.

I'd like to go back to another gathering I invited Karno and Christine; well, it was more like a special graduation dinner for these Aboriginal young men and women where he would actually bring culture to the ceremony. They absolutely loved it when Karno came because he would share so much Old Way wisdom and understandings.

We had some very, very high-profile military personnel present at some of these dinners. Karno always attended because his heart and soul was dedicated to our young people. He was all about watching wanting them to do well, wanting them to be successful, wanting them to not only succeed but excel. He would come and talk and address our young people. He'd bring culture in; he'd bring culture gear in with him. He'd teach and share, and it was a really wonderful relationship.

I still remember what happened at one particular ceremony when Karno said to me, would I be happy to do ceremony with him? And I said, absolutely. If you're happy to do it publicly I know I'm happy and so honoured. He invited me out in front of the general and all the public that were present, and it was being televised. And I actually went through a sacred feather ceremony with Karno. Now I've still got the feather. It's an eagle feather and such a ceremony does several things. First and foremost, I was extremely honoured and privileged because in Ramindjeri culture to go through feather ceremony with an eagle feather is the highest degree of respect that one tribal man can pay to another tribal man. And Karno did that with me, but in the process of that happening, he also gave me permission to carry both the Ramindjeri language and Dreaming. And that's what I do and still do today.

Steve: Do you want to talk about mum:mo:wee and perhaps explain what it actually means? Because Karno spoke about that constantly and I've heard that word many times, and I'm still not fully sure what it means. Would you like to give that some substance to this word please?

Colin: Karno, he formalized it, I think at a ceremony at Victor Harbor. But let me tell you it has been in Ramindjeri culture and dreaming since the beginning, and it is all about white fella and black fella coming together. Let me give you a personal and practical example of how this happened at one of the many Army ceremonies Karno attended when Karno presented to the then Chief of the Army this magnificent kangaroo skin. The General's Personal Assistant rung me before and said, look we would love to reciprocate with a gift for Uncle Karno. I agreed in stating that such an exchange of gifts is normal in the protocol of our culture. And I said, yes, there would be something that would be quite significant that I know Uncle Karno and his family would appreciate. And she said, what would that be? My suggestion was a set of duplicate medals for Uncle Arthur Walker.

And so, when Karno presented the kangaroo skin to the Chief of the Army, he presented to Karno, a magnificent set of medals. He gave him the duplicate medals and also a photograph of Uncle Arthur Walker.

Photo Description: Uncle Karno and Lieutenant General David Morrison A O at Muwerang (Kent Reserve, Victor Harbor, South Australia) with the exchange of gifts.

Photo Description: Uncle Karno and Lieutenant General David Morrison A O at Muwerang (Kent Reserve, Victor Harbor, South Australia) saluting the monument of the last known camping ground of the Ramindjeri.

But the General extended this gesture further. When I spoke to the P A, who was a colonel at the time, I said to her, could you please ask the chief if he would be happy to do the acknowledgement of country in Ramindjeri language? She said, how would we do that? I said, I believe that one of the highest signs of respect another person's culture is to speak their language.

Karno was absolutely overwhelmed. He was just so appreciative that the Chief of Army would speak Ramindjeri language on Ramindjeri land. I got the language and phonetically wrote it so that the chief would be able to speak it. And that is exactly what happened, the Chief of Army responded to Uncle Karno's welcome and did the acknowledgement in his language. And I believe that this was an absolute milestone. When you think about White men and Black men coming together, he is a white man, a very significant White man speaking Ramindjeri language on country. To me, that amplifies the whole essence of the spirit Wirritjin.

Steve: I'm going to ask a question which relates to one amazing ceremony Karno conducted. There is this ceremony, I've seen Karno give it twice and it's called the whispering song. He sort of starts whispering all the way through and I've noticed the impact it's had on people- it literally brings many to tears. Could you talk about that a bit, please?

Colin: I can't talk about it from Karno's perspective. But I can start this by first talking about smoking then move on to his whispering ceremony.

First up people need to understand, with the whole essence of smoking, I need to put a caveat in here, don't ever make assumptions that everyone does everything the same and it means the same. So, smoking for one mob and the way they do it and what they do is one thing and smoking for another mob and what they do and how they do it is another thing, and we don't ever assume that everybody is the same.

Now the way I do smoking is I make sure that I gather and collect the soil from the country. In my case all that gathering is very significant because we took soil from Australia to Gallipoli and mixed it with the soil at Gallipoli and that blend of soils came back to Australia and I've got that soil which was mixed with Ramindjeri soil and becomes a backdrop and companion to the actual smoking ceremony. With the smoke, it's about cleansing, first and foremost. So, its primary function is all about cleansing spirits. It has to be done with the right motives and the right spirit. Otherwise, it'll detract from what we're trying to achieve. It's all about respect, we're respecting the people, we're respecting the country and we're respecting creation.

Smoking, it's about cleansing before moving further into ceremony. From a white man's Perspective, it'd be something similar to perhaps if you were of the Christian faith, you do ceremony and you may do communion. They use bread and they have wine, and they go through a ceremony called the Sacrament and that is a part of their cleansing. Smoking has been around since forever, even in the Christian faith, they've had a type smoking through incense and a whole bunch of other stuff. So, let's just unpack this. So, we're really talking about cleansing. The second part of it is personal and is about me and when I do smoking, which from my perspective is all about healing. I think all of us need to be cleansed. I believe everyone needs healing. I'm not just talking about physically. I'm talking about spiritually; I'm talking about emotionally and I'm talking about mentally. We get hurt and people hurt us and that needs to be resolved before ceremony begins.

The last part of the smoking ceremony for me is about blessing, cleansing, healing and blessing. Once that is clear and present, we can now move on to the whispering sound. I believe he's singing a blessing. And he's singing, healing and blessing you all together, because everyone needs to hear a whisper. They do, don't they? Especially when it's Karno who is whispering.

Steve: That might explain why quite a few men start doing something they normally would never do in public; I've seen them crying.

Colin: It's, it's very powerful mate.

Steve: Isn't it?

Colin: We've seen it and we've felt it and for people who haven't seen and felt it, it's very hard to get across the impact it has. But I've seen grown men that I doubt ever have cried in publicly. You can see them doing this with their eyes and sort of putting their head down a bit to hide from the public gaze and you think, I know what you're doing. You can hide it if you want but he's got it out. It's like he's calling them inside and they don't even know what's happening to an extent. And it's very powerful. That's why with cleansing comes a healing that goes right through you.

You know, a lot of people believe that we are human beings, who are skin and bone who had a spiritual experience. I don't believe that. No. We are spiritual beings trapped in flesh and bone. We are beings who have a human experience.

And that is why it's so easy for our people to connect to creation through our ceremonies, it's our chance to talk to our spirits and our ancestors. We all do it in different ways, many go to a cemetery to pay respects to one of their ancestors who've passed. They speak to a hole in the ground with a concrete headstone with their name on it. The reality is it is just a bit of concrete. It's a block, but it's about what it represents.

And that's why our people and a lot of our young people need to reconnect to ceremony, smoking and even Karno's whispering song and his feather ceremony, that's where we need to be, we need to reconnect to our culture. We need to reconnect to our creation. We need to reconnect with each other. And there's been so many influences that have taken us so many of us away from all those things.

Steve: I want to share with you something that happened when Karno came to our place and did ceremony at our fire-pit. I told quite a few people in advance to try not to get caught up in Karno's gaze, because they may not quite be prepared for what's going to happen to them, I can see you are smiling when I said that, and I am fairly sure you know where this is going. Some people did look into Karno's eyes, and they all said the same thing. They said to me when he looked at me, he had this big smile on his face, but at the same time they felt like they were being completely undressed, as he was staring inside them and absolutely nothing was hidden. They all said it was like he'd read them completely and that of the secrets and all the things that were deposited deep within where his for the taking. It was something they'd never experienced before. They felt like there were no secrets when you were standing next to Karno.

Colin: I think the most important thing that comes out of that Steve is this, there is a discernment, a spiritual discernment, that some people do have, it's almost like an innate sixth sense. It's almost like that. And for some, it is very, very powerful and strong. But one of the things I will add to that is that what I loved about Karno is his ability as a lore man, as a leader, as a visionary and his talent in reading between our lines. He knew that everyone goes through a journey, and everyone's going to struggle and make mistakes.

I think one of the greatest attributes we can have in our human dimension which transforms into the spiritual dimension and that is to be, or try to be, nonjudgmental. See, that smirk and that smile when he is looking directly at and through you. It's almost like don't worry, mate. We've all been there before. It's almost like I know where you're coming from, and I know where you're going. I think one of the biggest things that is a problem for our mob and our people is that we condemn themselves. We are born in this flesh and for most of us we are very judgemental involving ourselves in finger pointing and looking at other people's problems and where they failed and what they did and shouldn't do. But here is the trick, we don't always get it right.

But the real truth is it is not about results, so long as you try to get it right, nothing else matters. The loreman's job is to assist us in journeying, and that's what Karno was doing when he was looking at you and others. He was digging deep within, and you knew you were being exposed and you knew the secrets were gone in front of him.

Steve: There was one observation, or maybe point of concern that someone who was also at the fire-pit when Karno was running that show, that I want to close with. Karno spent the whole night having a go at me and highlighting all my mistakes in front of others. Everyone including myself and Karno were laughing at my inadequacies and errors.

A friend approached me and remarked "God, how do you feel after all that?" "He spent all night having a go at you and laughing at you." I said, "honoured," which was not the reply he expected by a long shot. And I then said to him, "what did he actually say to you?" And he said, "Nothing."

We discussed this in more detail, and I pointed out that he spent the whole night teaching me with a smile on his face, and for me that night only has good memories.

Colin: Exactly, we've cracked it mate. I like the way we finished as Karno was always smiling, always teaching, and always walking between two worlds and always trying to show us how to get there.

Chapter Fourteen:

In Conversation (Part 2) - Colin Watego & Steven Strong

Steve: Are you familiar with Karno's skin group?

Colin: To an extent, but not fully, because I wanted to suss that out. Because with myself, I've got connections through kinship with other countries and other communities. I ended up catching up with Christine and I said to Christine in all my journeys with Karno, I can't ever remember him mentioning anything about skin.

But to begin with I'll give you my take on skin relationships so people can get an idea what this ancient tradition actually means. I posted a photo today that came in from ANZAC Day. And I want to talk about what happened at the coloured Diggers March. There were two men that went to Gallipoli with me. One of them was a Yolngu man from Arnhem Land and the other man came from the Wollembi.

Without going into the reasons why, together we went through ceremonies. And through these ceremonies we have become brothers. In other words, his skin is my skin, my skin is his.

His children are my children, my children are his children. Our grandchildren are part of this larger family network. Now our skin group and my skin group are identical.

Even though the details of Karno's skin are missing I can see this same synergy with him because even though you don't know these things when it happens, you still feel it and you know what it's about. It's like a spiritual sense that comes over you when you know when it's the right time because you know it's the right connection. And that was how it was with me and Karno. Both our totems are the eagle, so we are connected at that level.

But when comes to my skin brother from Arnhem Land, my totem, my skin has always been linked to water. So, I'm a saltwater person, freshwater person, I am a water person. it's really interesting when I spoke to my brother, from up there in Arnhem Land, his skin is, wut-wut which is the word for water. His skin is the same as my skin in terms of water.

Water is such an important part of Ramindjeri Dreaming and culture. You got the fresh water, the salt water, the lakes and the river systems.

So, returning to the question you asked regarding Karno's skin name when I spoke to Christine about it, her answer confirmed one aspect of his relationship to country and purpose, but extended into areas and realms totally unexpected. It turns out I was completely off-track in that the southern part of Australia does not recognise the notion of skins and as result of this vacuum Karno does not have a 'skin relationship' with anyone. His name Karno only adds to this lack of connection, his tribal name is Karnigi Ramindjeri which means "lucky warrior walking between two worlds." And the reality is his name itself performs the same function as skins, in that he could never marry of woman bearing the same ngartji (totem) name.

It obviously is water as well. The synergies between water and being anointed to walk between two worlds is as profound as it is mystifying The relationship between all of that leads to me now to a dimension that I hadn't given a lot of thought to before, but I'm thinking about now.

At the first level there is a shared connection. You see here I am on the east coast of Australia, both at the Northern Rivers in Bundjalung country, which is on the coast, and also the Torres Straits that's surrounded in water. Here I am also with my connection with my brother, Norman Day, who was an Elder a Loreman up in Arnhem land. And we all share the same skin group water. And here I am with my brother, Karno in the most southern part of Australia which is where the full water systems all the southern half of Australia all come together and that it just generates a powerful feeling of connectivity. I just can't escape the fact that everything's linked together but particularly in light of the Ramindjeri story of Wirritjin Dreaming story black man and white man coming together as one in peace.

That sort of explains when I actually thought about all of that, why Karno's skin name, which is all about family and who is allowed to become family, was actually Karno. And that is his skin name because his birth certificate name was Lancelot Gilbert Walker. I didn't know what it was. He is bearing what those in the North of Australia would refer to as his skin name, but it really is his given name. But it is much more than that in his case, because as we know, Karno is men's business, he is women's business and is also everybody's business.

Steve: Tell me about the times Karno became actively involved with you when you were still in the army.

Colin: When we were doing the defence stuff, there was one particular mention that needs to be made and that is during our PRC graduations. We would invite Karno and Christine and other VIP guests to come along to see our young Aboriginal Torres Strait Island men and women graduate, and they would attend their graduation dinner.

At one of these dinners, we had the patron for army, the Indigenous patron for army at the time was a very lovely man, a great leader by the name of Major General Michael Fairweather. So, I invited Karno to do some ceremonies after the dinner and he bought all of his gear, and he also bought his kangaroo skin, and the young people loved it simply because he was teaching culture Old Way, in a very formal setting, but in an informal way.

Karno also took it upon himself at the ceremony at the appropriate time to invite the general out to the front and he presented him with an amazing message stick. That sacred message stick was presented to the general. Now, the general asked me a very important question. He said, "Col, I'm not sure that I can receive this stick and you know, because of the proprietary of gifts and whatever is given can be misconstrued as a bribe or inducement."

And I said to the I said to the general with total respect. I said, "Sir, you can't not accept the gift. No, you can't say no."

I said, "This is a proper ceremony going on here. The fact that you've been identified by Karno who is an extremely honourable Elder who wanted to acknowledge your presence and intentions. Karno is a Loreman and a visionary leader. It would be my recommendation that you actually receive the gift and the spirit in which it's intended."

After explaining the Old Way protocol and obligations that are intertwined the general felt much more comfortable in receiving the message stick. Now the general has since passed, but I am aware that he had donated that message stick to one of the museums, but I'm not sure which one it went to,

This again is another demonstration of the spirit of Wirritjin and how it was exercised at the highest levels of leadership. It was during this type of ceremony and many other ceremonies I would catch up with Karno and Christine out at Salisbury North, whenever I got the chance to go and visit them. And I always did whenever I was in Adelaide or in the area. It was a chance to sit down and have a cuppa and a good old yarn. And we'd just share information and talk about the challenges of our young people and our old people.

Karno had such a great spirit and always fought for justice, but not just here. I remember him showing me a letter once that was written to high-ranking people and it was not even about Australia. It was all about New Caledonia and Christine would know a lot more about this, I only had a brief outline of the issues that worried him. But the injustice of what was happening to their people over there at that time concerned him greatly, which also speaks reams about the spirit kangaroo is about teaching and the emu is intrinsically tied into issue about law and behind Uncle Karno Walker. Wirritjin connects all mobs, doesn't it, it brings together all mobs doesn't matter where they are. It's a global thing, isn't it? It's not just a thing that happens in Adelaide or South Australia, it's about everyone coming together as one.

And one of the great things about being involved in the military pathway programs is that we had young people from cultures all over Australia and the Torres Straits. So, there was this ongoing sharing, training and teaching, and I and I don't think a lot of people really understand the magnitude of the influence that Karno culturally delivered safely and appropriately to so many young people.

Now after some time, we were leading in towards the 100th anniversary of the remembering of, of ANZAC and I remember talking to Karno and saying, look it's really deep in my spirit that I'm going to present something very spiritual and so Old Way to the new Chief of Army and when I spoke to Karno about my plans that were still in the making and somewhat undefined. All I knew was that the military personnel to be involved in that presentation were Aboriginal, and I felt the ceremony was all about honouring warrior spirit. It came on my spirit to approach Karno and because I had already gone through ceremony with Karno, I needed his advice and guidance.

I remember sitting at the kitchen table at Karno's place and, of course, Aunty Christine was there, and I said to him, "I have been asked to make a presentation to the new chief of army who was Lieutenant General Angus Campbell. I thought about the earlier induction you helped me with and what stood out was that these other men that I had selected who came from all over Australia. I'm from the very east in Bundjalung country. We had men from the north of the top of Australia, a man from Tasmania, others from the west. So, we've covered the, the full width and breadth of Australia.

But it spanned further in location and timing, there was a relative, a very good friend of mine, Uncle Glenn Waters, who was the great nephew of Uncle Lenny Waters, who was our very first Aboriginal fighter pilot. He was a Kamilaroi man, and their tribe is situated inland to the west of New South Wales. That rollcall included an Eora Elder by the name of John Angel Hands who was involved in planning for Gallipoli ceremony. And I also had Uncle Darren Moffett an amazing Eora artist who I'd worked with for many years. Together this mob spread all over the continent, and I wanted to honour that spread of people and Old Way wisdom.

When I spoke to Karno about these great people I wanted to encapsulate a dream, the Dreaming story and the imagery needed. We agreed that an artist of great skill and high sensitivity was required which led back to Darren Moffett who lives in Albury Wodonga. Because he and I had already worked on other projects, particularly around art, Dreaming and stories, we felt he was the obvious choice. The way we saw this brief was that it's not only spiritual story but includes a journey of our people before today that continues on to tomorrow.

This magnificent artwork which encapsulated important symbols that created one very important narrative. It definitely had the kangaroo and emu front and centre. They are really iconic totems and these sacred symbols for our people and for many of our peoples and tribes. The kangaroo is about teaching and the emu is intrinsically tied into issue about law and 'as on top' business.

The serpent is also part of this Aboriginal narrative which starts at the base and contours up the didgeridoo (yidaki) towards the top. Our ancestors, the kangaroo and the emu are depicted on either side and their footprints accompany the serpent. Towards the top, towards the head of the serpent, were kangaroo and emu footprints, which were white then turned black. All the symbols and motif merge at the top where the sun, which is the symbol for army, is positioned.

Amongst the ochre-coloured dot artwork is an eagle which represented Air Force and, and at the base of the tail is a dugong. When Uncle Darren was commissioned to do some artwork for the Navy Royal Australian Navy in recognition of 100 years of Indigenous or First Nations contribution to the Navy, I sat on a committee with him when he was deliberating over the content included in this magnificent artwork called The Salute. He said to me, during his initial drafting, he did a picture of a whale, which when I think about it, it would have been awesome been because this aquatic mammal was a major totem of the Ramindjeri. But upon further reflection I said to Darren, "Look mate, that'd be great, but we need to understand that although the whale is the totem for so many of our mobs in mainland Australia, we need a totem that represents both Australia and the Torres Straits tribes. And I said that could be the dugong.

So, he changed the artwork to the dugong. However, we still had other symbols representing many different tribes and granted we didn't have them all, but we had had a lot.

And then there was the serpent itself, which was blue, meaning water, life and sustainability. But there was more to it, the land totems and water totems within the blue serpent. In combination, Karno and I felt it symbolised a spirit of bringing everyone together, of black men and white men coming together in peace.

The pascal colours in the artwork on the yidaki were all about the future and right at the top of the artwork is the sacred constellation, the Southern Cross. Many of our mobs know that the significance of those stars.

When we did the final ceremony in July, myself and Darren (Karno's nephew and representative) presented this artwork to the then Chief of Army in Canberra at the Royal Military College at Duntroon. Then as the appointed custodian of the artwork it came back to me.

Oh, I forgot to mention there were also two boomerangs in this painting. One representing Nampa boomerangs in Nampa language, and the other represented an emu. They were fighting boomerangs, and they all travelled as a package together throughout the country.

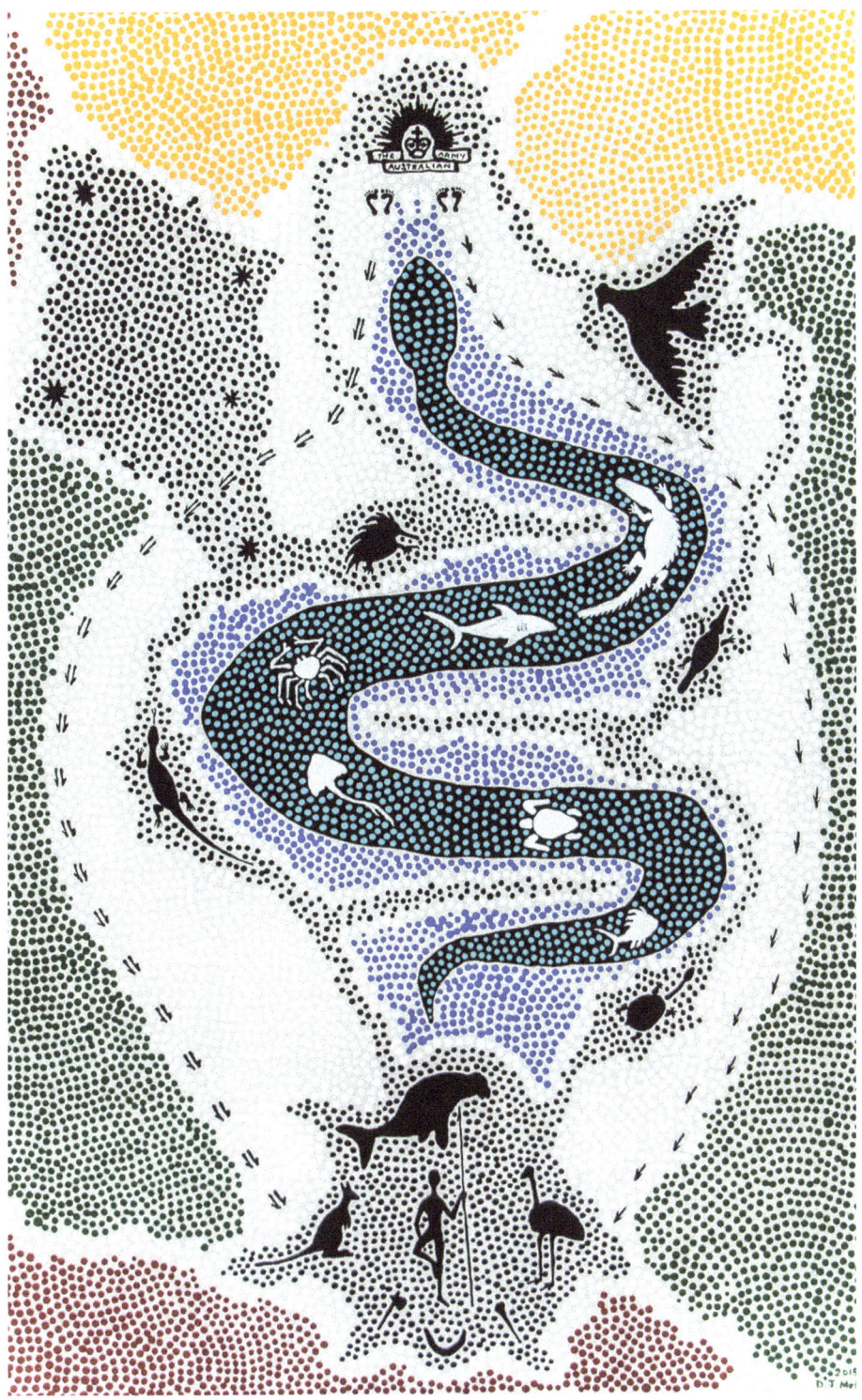

Photo Descripton: Original (Indigenous) warriors at Anzac Cove Gallipoli for the Department of Defence's Honouring Warrior Spirit ceremony.

On one occasion when we did a ceremony on country in Canberra, I collected soil at Kent Reserve Victor Harbour, Ramindjeri Ruwe (Country) and also from the lone pine tree. Near the Australian War Memorial, then that soil was taken with us with all of our Aboriginal and Torres Strait Islander artifacts to Gallipoli. That's where we did ceremony on the banks of ANZAC Cove at Gallipoli. I had the absolute pleasure of spreading the Australian soil into the sand at Gallipoli and then scooped up the mixture of sand and soil to bring it back to Australia.

After we returned from there in August, we did another very important ceremony at the Australian War Memorial, where the soil was then respectfully spread around the base of the lone pine tree which sits on the outskirts of the Memorial. It now rests in the memorial grounds and some of that soil was given to Christine accepting it on behalf of Karno and the Ramindjeri peoples. But it's outside and the intention is that anyone can go to the lone pine tree and grab a small handful of that soil because many people have lost loved ones and relation. But it's not just for those who fell and died on the battlefields, some survived and came back broken and hurt and their families suffered as well. They too can take that soil back to their own country, wherever that may be and spread that soil and do ceremony on their own country.

After this returning ceremony of three soils, I presented the artwork back to the Australian Army and since then, it has travelled around in certain places. I think at the moment it might even be at the Australian War Memorial or they might be in Canberra, The yidaki and artwork travel as a set. The Dreaming story that inspired the artwork will always belong to the Ramindjeri.

Such sacred items are so important to our culture and Dreaming and I believe one of the biggest problems we have today for Aboriginal people today is they're not getting ceremony. Karno has said this so many times. We've got to bring ceremony back everywhere.

Steve: You know that Karno wanted all these sacred rocks I am the custodian of so they could do ceremony, and everyone could come back on Ramindjeri country and do rock ceremony and bring culture and Dreaming back front and centre and on two occasions the government stepped in and stopped us, but they're not going to stop us. But we'll get it through eventually. But that is another story.

Colin: Yes, it is, but this what Karno wanted, and it will happen, it has to. In the meantime, I am traveling all over Australia as we speak. And I'm carrying the language and those artifacts and everywhere I go with all the stuff that we do in communities. The story gets told because it is just so important to talk about the spirit and this is what I get to keep coming back to, it is all about Wirritjin. Karno never let up talking about the Black-fella White-fella Dreaming that is coming and coming soon.

Colin Watego

Chapter Fifteen:

Crossing the Divide - Steven Strong

At some time soon after my opening chapter was written and read by Christine we were talking on the phone about the contents and literally out of nowhere Christine made mention of Karno's interaction and request to a colony of ants. I actually knew the location of the ants, as I remembered Karno taking me past the anthill and vaguely remember him mentioning something about himself and another spending some time there. Details about who that was and what took place was never given then, but now was a different equation and Christine certainly filled in some of the gaps.

But certainly not all the gaps and past what did happen, there were some massive questions remaining that could never be answered. Christine told me that about week before an ant ceremony Karno found a dead goanna and took it to the anthill and placed it on top. Within an hour nothing remained bar the bones, the ants are very big (about two centimetres in length) and each had a large set of pincers. I do remember looking at them and being extremely careful and wary in relation to getting too close, but that was when I was there, and different rules and instructions applied when Karno took Wirritjin to the same location. Wirritjin (Stephen Robinson) was given that name by Karno, he had been with him for a considerable time before I came onto the scene and this time around it wasn't a goanna corpse that was positioned on the anthill, but a living breathing Homo sapien that was told to stand on the hill and await further instructions.

When told to step forward, Karno began to sing which was accompanied by his clapsticks, and so the ceremony began. For quite some time to follow Wirritjin stood motionless on the mound, and not once was he bitten. By Christine's reckoning close to half an hour passed before Karno asked Wirritjin to sit down. As Wirritjin has since passed over, I have no way to ask what his reaction was, but while standing on top of the mound is a huge ask in itself, to sit down must have been a real test of trust and absolute belief in the magic of Karno's song. It was warranted, as Wirritjin did not get bitten once while was sitting or standing while Karno was singing.

As amazing as this event Christine described was, it had not reminded me of what I had omitted from my earlier account. It was what Christine added next in response to my question as to what and how he sang to the ants. She told me that such contact was never restricted to insects but ascended much further up the pyramid of life. While the ant contact was limited to this ceremony, when it came to kangaroos, that was a common occurrence. Christine told me that Karno would often go out in the morning to the front paddock and sit next to the kangaroos. They would gather around him and engage in conversation; such was the depth of interaction he would often break into laughter after one had 'spoken' to him. She had no doubt whatsoever that both Karno and the kangaroos were making sense to each other and clearly passing on information.

That was when the 'bells starting ringing.' Almost immediately the chain of events through a phone call made by Karno over three thousand kilometres away was front and centre and demanded both acknowledgement and an audience. I began by apologising to Christine for forgetting such a memorable event, then began to fill in the gaps.

Separated by Three Thousand Kilometres and Four Hours.

We were nearing a cave Klaus Dona had detected through the use of technology I did not fully understand, but since this was the fourth time we had inspected sites marked out on the map he compiled, and on every occasion, we had found something sacred and special, it was because of this perfect 'track-record' we did expect to find something.

For the first time while on site in the Gosford region, Aunty Beve was unwell and did not smoke us before setting off. Knowing that entering or even approaching any sacred site must be done through respecting Original protocol, I decided to conduct a ceremony that was given to me by Uncle Jerry Bostock, which he had used whenever on country. I mistakenly assumed if it was good enough for him, the same would apply to us.

So, we went onto the site and when we got fairly close to the cave Klaus had highlighted, I went ahead and built a small rock cairn. Past that construction I announced my presence and intentions then called the others over to each add another rock and introduce themselves. Evan was first-in-line and in what seemed to be a promising start as he approached the stacked rocks, a brown owl flew out of the cave and shed one feather which Evan picked up. We all saw this as an affirming gift, and that optimism was only reinforced by both the ochre paintings on the cave walls and the accidental filming of white orbs. On one occasion we filmed one such orb as it moved towards one of the party (Sean), then stopped as it neared him and changed direction running up his arm and around his head. That was not due to anything random but was clear proof of intent and awareness of where he was. It did seem as we left the site with an owl feather in hand and film of orbs moving and avoiding, that this had been a successful investigation.

Four hours later Evan came up to me with his mobile in hand and a concerned expression when telling me that Karno had rung and wanted to talk to me. We both knew this was not a good sign, with one earlier exception whenever Karno wanted to talk to me that wish was relayed by a third party, which on most occasions was his wife, Christine. Knowing that the only other time Karno rang was because he was annoyed, verging on angry, over something he thought I had done, Evan handed his mobile to me expecting the worst.

He was right in assuming it was bad news but both of us never thought it was this bad. Karno began his remonstration with what seemed a calm opening gambit by asking, "Did you go onto country today?"

"Yes, but it was on Darkinyooong country, and we had Aunty Beve's permission to do so." Karno was ringing from the Ramindjeri Culture Centre situated some three thousand kilometres to the south-west, and I had no need to get his blessings as we had always done any archaeology there via Aunty Beve. At this stage in proceedings, I could not see a problem here and thought perhaps I had misread his motivation for ringing or asking.

"Yes, I know you got permission to enter, but did you smoke yourself and the others?"

"Well, no. but Aunty Beve is unwell and couldn't smoke us, so I used a ceremony Uncle Jerry gave me …"

I did intend to fully explain what that ceremony entailed, but Karno cut me off in mid-sentence. "You mean the rock stacking ceremony where you announced who you were and why you came?"

That threw me, I was totally caught off-guard by what he said and moreover, how he could possibly know of my change in protocol, but it got worse. Before I could offer any response, he added two more what should have been unknowns into this mix. "So, Evan picked up the feather from the owl, and why were you wearing a red T-shirt in the bush?"

Both questions, although seemingly unrelated were utterly factual. Evan did pick up the feather and I was wearing the same red shirt as I spoke to him. I was way out of my depth here, and had a lot of trouble assembling a reply, but that certainly wasn't a problem for Karno. "When I gave you ceremony you were smoked, and I told you that is what you must do whenever on country. The Spirits have told me that if you ever go onto country and do not smoke yourself, you will not leave, they will kill you. They are not happy about this, and Evan picking up that feather, what did he make of that?"

Finally, I had a chance to speak instead of being overwhelmed with how and why. "He took it as a good sign, a positive omen."

"Did he? Well, he got that wrong he should have left it where it fell. He will get sickness and it will be for some time, you both broke Old Way protocol and Law and there will have to be consequences." (Evan was sick almost continually for the next two years, and we have never gone onto country since without smoking ourselves first).

How …

There was more to this phone call, but the main points have been addressed. However, throughout the conversation one question remained constant. How did he know this, we were separated by a distance of three-thousand kilometres and four hours in timing. All that was said by Karno was right and precise and once he finished his critique, I had to ask one final question. "Karno we are so far apart, and I know you weren't in the bush watching, so how do you know everything we did and said?"

"The owl left and told another, and that was passed on until the red kangaroo sitting on my veranda was told. And he told me everything."

I had no idea what he was going to say in response to my question, but never, ever, would I have predicted a response like this. This message travelled at a speed of seven-hundred and fifty kilometres per hour for four hours. No bird, marsupial or any other animal can move that fast, and when comes to present-day realities, how can a bird, communicate in such detail with any marsupial. None of this Original package fits into any scientific explanation or narrative.

Regardless, Karno was on the phone telling me what we did, wore and said and he was three thousand kilometres away when this happened. What it comes down to in the simplest of terms is that Karno does not do science, he does Old Way magic.

A Stick in Time and Place

I felt it appropriate to close with another mystical truth and this time Karno was not the principal agent, it is all about Karno's talking stick, a photograph of which is on the back cover. When I came down to Ramindjeri country the first time, I had no idea for how long or what would eventuate. Over a week passed before Karno, Peter and others decided it was possibly time to give both myself and Darren ceremony, but in doing so another Old Way authority had to make the final decision.

It wasn't a bird, kangaroo or Elder they had to liaise and consult with, but a piece of wood. Sacred, special and bearing many carvings, this talking stick was to be the final arbitrator. Karno came up to me and first up grabbed my black folder from which I had been taking notes and threw it away, stating that "you won't need this." He then replaced the folder with his talking stick and told me to hold it for next hour, and when he came back the stick would decide whether I was worthy of this honour. Fortunately, I did pass stick-muster and the ceremony was given, the details of which are secret and private, but the point being my character was not assessed by an exam, interview or some form questioning, but a magic stick.

Anyone that knew Karno well, would never doubt or contest that he was a Clever-fella and practitioner of Old Way magic. And right now, what he said, what he did and what he knew is sadly lacking throughout the planet and so essential in the days soon to come. From our perspective Karno is as good as it gets and a role model that is essential in the times of dramatic change and Earthly ascension that are so near and so desperately needed.

Conclusion:

Steven Strong

Granted as none of us "walk between two worlds," all we could ever realistically aim for in this book is 'near enough.' Nevertheless, we believe what we did muster up is a sufficient overview. The only certainty that can never be disputed was Karno's often stated claim that whenever he did pass over, he would and could do more on the other side than while he was incarnated into flesh and bone.

What is a constant factor in any recount of Karno's life and deeds is the ever-present role of the very non-scientific concept of magic. And that is his greatest blessing, and conversely, an empirical curse. Pragmatists, atheists, sceptics and many who champion science as the final arbitrator, will immediately scoff and derisively dismiss such nonsense. They will claim that either he is being deceitful and manipulative, or that those who testify to such mystical extensions are lying or naïve in the extreme. Even though ten people, including Graham Hancock and his wife Santha, were present when Karno disappeared, these armchair critics who were not in attendance at this vanishing will put this all down to a clever ruse or a deliberate lie. Their same rules of exclusion will apply to every other documented miraculous claim, but in every case bar none their denial demands that either Karno or all witnesses were being dishonest and mischievous. It all comes to one of two options; someone is lying, or we are all telling the truth.

The fundamental scientific flaw in their obstinance is that most scientist also subscribe to the Big Bang Theory. They will give an exact figure as to when out of sheer nothingness a huge explosion took place that created all life and a multitude of stars and constellations. In the simplest terms what they are agreed upon as an incontestable scientific fact is that out nothing everything was created, but as yet have not duplicated this equation in any laboratory. To create something out of nothing is magic, pure and simple, there is no other way of categorising such a seminal event, life did not exist then it did. If that is the agreed scientific starting point throughout the Universe, then surely one person tinkering at the esoteric edges through vanishing for a short period of time then reappearing, is no more than a minor version of more of the same.

From my standpoint the real issue here is not about if this actually happened but is more about the only discrepancy in the many reports of what we saw, the timing. Christine, Unbulara, Darren, my son Evan, myself and another who was there, agree completely about every event except how long the gap was between Karno disappearing and then further on reappearing when standing behind his wife, Christine. Ten seconds, twenty, half a minute, close to a minute, a full minute, and in my case over a minute are the times offered by each of us, none are the same. As to why there is no consensus on the time taken is an issue that has no definitive concluding remark or explanation. Whether when Karno entered the portal time slowed down, stood still or variations on that theme affected us in different ways, is hard to pin down to the second. But the trick with assessing any magical manifestation, is that when walking between two worlds, clocks and the here and now are irrelevant. On the other side time does not exist, so trying to quantify something that only exists here, but not there, is a tenuous exercise at best.

Irrespective of whatever verdict those who were never there do cobble together, the overriding truth that Karno was indeed a "warrior that walks between two worlds" and nothing any expert nor authority denies will change or ameliorate that eternal truth. When it comes to Old Way wisdom, ceremonies or magic, Karno is undeniably first amongst equals and when pressed for an explanation he was adamant that what he did was nothing unusual or miraculous. As he said when pressed for an explanation, it was all a matter of finding the portal, which is something we could all do, if only we knew how and where to look. What some of us occasionally glimpse out of the corner of our eye Karno can see front and centre all day long.

This book is our attempt at both honouring an exceptional practitioner of Old Ways, and presenting a role model as to what is needed for who lead once this planet completes its cleansing and ascension. What we have today when it comes to Presidents, Prime Ministers and dictators share one consistency, they are poor choices who lack the vision, empathy and real understanding as to why we exist and are incarnate on this planet. Whether separately or in combination, if compared to Karno they fall short at every possible level. His story is our story, and could yours too, all we have to do is embrace the land, the Guardian Spirits, the Dreaming and most importantly Wirritjin, once past that leap of faith, the rest is easy.

Acknowledgements:

Apart from those who knew Karno and put together a written response, we also wish to thank David for assisting Christine in the collection and placement of the many photographs of Karno into this book. We want to apologise to the many other people who had a close relationship with Karno that we did not directly approach. It was not a matter of picking and choosing, but simply due to the reality that once we had covered most angles and examples of Karno's words and deeds, there was no need to expand or elaborate further.